The Thinking Cure

PROGRAM YOUR MIND
FOR SUCCESS AND HAPPINESS

The Thinking Cure

PROGRAM YOUR MIND FOR SUCCESS AND HAPPINESS

DAVID PITCOCK

www.thethinkingcure.com

©Copyright 2012 - David Pitcock

Contents

Thanks and Acknowledgments..7

Introduction 9

Feeling Good 13

Your Guided Missile..25

Defining Your Dreams and Goals 37

Finding the Good in Everything 45

Hang Ups..53

The Thinking Cure 61

Five Minutes to Learn and a Lifetime to Master 69

How Do I Practice Perfectly Every Day?..77

How to Mindweave and Put It All Together 87

From the Author...93

THANKS AND ACKNOWLEDGMENTS

When you take on a project such as writing a book and attempting to offer things that can help people you really start to think of the people that have made a difference in your life. It would be impossible to list them all here, but if I miss you, and I have ever met you, know that you are in this list.

First and foremost my wife, Barb Pitcock. I've never in my life met another girl like her. She has more zest for life and authentic love and hope for other people than anyone I've ever met. She is my best friend, my hero and the mom to our three amazing kids. She has taught me so much.

To my kids Brooklyn, Chance and Kali. We have been on this journey together for as long as you have been alive. I know there are times when I was growing and learning and I hope you respect me for that. I hope you have learned that your only limitations are in your mind, and they can be overcome in a matter of seconds. My hope is that you see your dad as a dreamer and I hope the lessons we have learned together will make you all stronger. I have learned so much from each one of you and I can't wait to keep learning! You all three are so different, you are all on my list of heroes in my life.

To my parents. I wrote about you some in this book. A few real stories and real things that happen in people's lives. I wanted people to know that it's okay when crap happens. I want you to both know that I have you both on pedestals in my life that no one can reach. In all the adversity I have become a better man. What else can a son ask of his parents? Thank you for being you.

To all of the amazing dreamers, speakers, authors, teachers and mentors in my life. You lit a path for me to follow in many times of darkness in my life. One of the greatest teachers I've listened to is Kevin

Trudeau. I've heard him say from stage a dozen times or more, "I just hope one person gets it." I am working on being that one person Kevin, thank you.

To my best friend Bert Leach. You were the first person to hand me that set of Jim Rohn tapes almost 20 years ago. You inspired me in ways you will never know. Most importantly, you taught me what a best friend really means in life.

Introduction

A thought that repeatedly goes on in my head is, "Are you afraid of being happy? Or are you just addicted to being in a rut?" Read this a few times and it pretty much sums up how people live in every area of their lives…right in the middle somewhere, not sure, confused and asking questions.

What is *The Thinking Cure* and how is this different than the thousands of personal development and self help books on the market today? I will answer these questions in this book. But let me give you a few bullet points to get your blood flowing.

We talk about *The Thinking Cure* and Mindweaving in this book. It is not that they are synonymous, The Thinking Cure is the entire process and Mindweaving is what you are actually doing to string a line of good thoughts together to actually make them a reality. Most people have a great thought and then their mind tells them why that can't be great. Most people think happy and then go right back to sad, mad or shy. Most people have a great idea only to be reminded that it won't work… Mindweaving is putting the good string of thoughts together and eliminating the old programs.

Imagine going to a seminar or buying a DVD set on how to lose weight, get toned up and get in better shape. They tell you all the reasons why this is all great and you are agreeing and getting excited. Then the course ends and they have never shown you any exercises or the fact that YOU NEED TO GET ON THE TREADMILL! There are thousands of programs like that in the self help industry. *The Secret* is a common book that surely helped a lot of people understand what the law of attraction is all about. There is no WORK to do in that entire book…it's not going to work as far as creating action and results in your life. If you want to learn about the law of attraction, it is a terrific book. If you want to apply it in your life and get real results, it isn't.

The Thinking Cure is about having a thought, creating some action and getting the results. Thought, action, results. It is really that simple and it should be. The simplicity of this book is refreshing. How to get or be anything you really want. This book will show you how to think the good thoughts that create whatever you want, how to remove the negative commands and blocks that hold you back every day, how to overcome the physical and mental hang ups in less than a minute and, of course, how to give each of your thoughts the energy they need to become real. You sit down and eat lunch every day…you thought it, took action and ate. Any of the goals in your life can be accomplished the same way. You just need a mind makeover so you know how easy it really is. Plus, you need to know that most of the negative stuff in your mind was CREATED by you or by someone in AUTHORITY and they are stopping you. *The Thinking Cure* will dissolve the negative stuff.

You want more money, a better relationship, a better attitude, more friends, a new house or just to help a bunch of people…why aren't you getting every single one of them? It is your thinking, I promise. Once I learned this, my life changed dramatically! I've been in your shoes, I've applied everything in this book and I've gotten the results. You just have programs playing in your mind and hang ups in your life that are stopping you. If you don't take care of this right now, it will just keep on going and you will be oblivious and continue to live knowing there is something missing.

I lived with those thoughts and that attitude that held me back, made me afraid, embarrassed, shy, broke, depressed and a host of other negative feelings. I have spent over 20 years listening to teachers, mentors, speakers and coaches at a huge monetary expense. I appreciate each of them in their own way more than I'll ever be able to show and I know every penny spent was more than worth it. This book is putting 20 years of personal development in bite size pieces that give you results. Real results. Not just advice. You can get advice from anyone and most of it you get that person has NOT been through what you are going through or facing, and worse yet, they have never applied the things they teach in their lives. I work in this every day of my life still.

Luckily I had a mentor who was 10 percent words and 90 percent action and result oriented…I want to pass on to you what I believe everyone should be taught in school and a hundred years from now will probably be the norm. I struggled setting goals and achieving them for awhile, but once I knew the real recipe, I never looked back. I've gone from broke, bankrupt and down on my luck to owning three multi-million dollar businesses and still cranking! My relationships are things I cherish and love now and I know whatever goal I set, I will achieve. Most importantly, I'm happy and feel good every single day. There was a time in my life when I had none of the above. I want you to feel that way too! *The Thinking Cure* is not some rah rah cheer leader program. There are thousands of those. They motivate you for as long as you are listening and then you are back to the real world. I have most of them in my library. *The Thinking Cure* is about thinking, acting and getting the results. Period. I want to make an important side note here. I talk some in this book about my successes and the large businesses we have built. I talk about money because it is easy to measure. If I say, "Hey, how happy are you?" That is hard to answer. But if I say, "How much money are you making?" I can measure that. I don't care if you make $40,000 a year, a month or a week. You can be the happiest, most successful person on the planet. Please understand my passion for wealth may be different than yours, but these are my experiences and that is why I share them. You don't have to have a ton of money to be happy and successful…it just sure feels good.

I believe with all my heart and soul and the results in my life that *The Thinking Cure* can help you answer some of those hard questions. Why am I here? What am I supposed to do? What happens now? And how do I get some of that stuff? I will warn you, if you think to yourself when reading this book, "Man, this sounds way to easy," it is because the concept is! Remember though, sometimes the things that are easy in life are also easy not to do.

It is said it is about the journey and not the destination. I hope once you reach that destination you immediately start another journey. I encourage you to visit www.thethinkingcure.com and get all the free information you can. I hope this book helps you KEEP YOUR DREAMS ALIVE!

David Pitcock

Chapter 1

Feeling Good

I remember it so well. It was a summer day on a weekend in Kansas in 1976. I was six years old and had a green Schwinn bike with the banana seat. I know it was a weekend as my dad worked every other day and wasn't home during the day. I would ride that bike with training wheels up and down the block on Oakdale Street where I grew up. Later in the evenings I would ride along the sidewalk and listen to the locusts buzzing in the trees. I liked to try to look in the trees and see their wings moving while they were singing. I also picked all of the dead locust skins off the trees and kept them. I know my mom appreciated this. On this specific day though, something was about to be different. There were no training wheels on my bike. My dad was running behind me as I had crashed many times before. But this time was different...my dad let go and I stayed on two wheels and just kept on riding! I could ride a bike! Even though I'd fallen a dozen times before, something kept me getting on that bike.

The feeling at that moment of complete freedom and overcoming was amazing. It seems though, I've had more of the feelings of despair, sadness and loss of hope than those incredible feelings of complete freedom and being in control. In my travels and experiences I understand most people feel bad more than they feel good. In my travels and talks I've learned that most people are still riding that bike of life with training wheels and are either afraid to take them off, have had someone tell them they could never ride without them or just don't want to get hurt again when they fall off.

This book is about how to have more of those amazing feelings of complete control over everything in your life as opposed to great despair. It's really a simple recipe that hardly anyone applies. We know the formula as we were born with it. It taught us to walk. It taught us how to know when we are hungry and when we are tired. We have an internal mechanism inside that simply knows what feeling good is all about. If we would just get out of its way…we can feel good all of the time. There are hundreds of books that are written with these success principles. I spent twenty years reading books, applying these techniques, attending seminars, watching documentaries on quantum physics and seeing real results in my life. I just had never seen it written or taught in a way that anyone could apply it. That is what Mindweaving and *The Thinking Cure* are all about.

It's like when you buy a new computer, it is clean and runs perfectly. Eventually it gets bogged down with bad commands and programs. You just need to clean it off. That is what *The Thinking Cure* will do for you. It gives you a method at any time in your life to remove a bad program… and shows you how to tell there is one running.

The Timeline

This is something I talk a lot about in live seminars and coaching. We all have a timeline that started when we were born and stops when we die. Like my bike riding experience, we all have good memories. Unfortunately most people never use those memories to build new ones. Instead we look at our timeline of when we were five years old and our parents started to put things in our head. At eight years old teachers and relatives started to add their opinions to the mix. At twelve and fourteen we had friends, peers, coaches and more teachers putting things in our heads. When we turned eighteen we had professors and bosses. The older we get the more we listen and believe the media and so called gurus on how to live our lives. At the age of fifty-five we have the doctors and infomercials telling us what diseases we have and how many prescription medications we need. It seems that at every point in our lives we have outside sources putting things in our heads and we never ask ourselves IF THEIR OPINIONS ARE OKAY OR WHAT

WE BELIEVE! This makes it difficult later when we get excited about something and want to accomplish things. We have bad programs that we and others have created running in our minds.

Ask yourself this. In a 24 hour day are you happy and feeling good all 24 hours? When I counsel and ask people at our live seminars this most people are lucky to have one hour during the day that makes them feel good! That is the goal of *The Thinking Cure*. Let's turn that gap around. Let's feel good 23 hours and 55 minutes of everyday, and the other five minutes when bad programs creep in, let's cancel and fix them immediately and get on with feeling good. Feeling good all of the time is the goal! That is when you create and THAT is when the law of attraction works in your favor.

At the age of 23 I started to learn about this recipe for success. Over the last twenty years I have spent hundreds of thousands of dollars on audios, books, seminars with gurus, coaching and more. What I want this book and Mindweaving to give you is twenty years of knowledge in however long it takes you to read this book!

The rest of my life's mission is to make sure people understand that success does not have to be hard! Success and feeling good can be yours every day, every hour and every minute. It is possible to take every situation in your life and make it work for you and not against you. Sound too good to be true? That is one of the things that will hold you back. Your thinking! Mindweaving will show you how to take your thoughts and keep them moving in the right direction so good things happen to you! In essence, how to weave several good thoughts together and start your mental thought processes to going in the right direction.

Have you ever met someone who simply is lucky? It seems everything they touch turns to gold. Well, they have a secret, it is how they think. Whether they know it or not, their thoughts are attracting things and not repelling them. What do your thoughts do?

A Lesson from my Grandfather

When I was very young my grandfather would bring me little things from where he worked. They were machinery parts, metal things, batteries of some sort and magnets. I've been fascinated with magnets since I was a very little kid. I remember specifically having two magnets about the size of a Fig Newton cookie. My grandfather handed them to me and said, "I'll give you five dollars if you can put these two ends together." I would sit there for hours trying to put the two negative ends of those magnets together and wondering, "How in the world can I not get these two pieces of metal to touch?" They were tiny pieces of metal but no matter how hard I tried I simply could not get them to touch. My grandfather would just laugh. Magnets are amazing. When you put a positive and negative end together they literally pull themselves towards one another. When you put the two negative ends or positive ends together they will never touch. The energy is mind boggling in that tiny piece of iron. We do this exercise at the Mindweaving live seminars and it still amazes people how powerful something that small can be.

I read a book by Dr. David Hawkins titled *Power vs. Force*. It helped me understand why people stay the way they are and no matter how hard they try, they can never get the things they want or become the person they want. He was talking about how emotions are measured energetically. He also shared how each thought that we have can actually be measured in microwatts! Yes, our thoughts actually contain energy that goes out into the world! Think about this. If you are angry, then you are putting out anger energy and guess what you get back? The millions of people that also have angry thoughts will gladly share their angry thoughts with you. If you are full of love, peace and hope then those thoughts have certain energy as well. In other words, what you are putting out there, you are getting in here. Whenever you hear someone talk about the law of attraction again, just know they are talking about the thousands of thoughts you are having everyday and what they are doing to you. How many people do you know that WANT things to be different so badly. They don't want to be in their current situation anymore! Yet all they talk about or think about are the same negative things they always have. They are attracting, just like the magnet, all of the other thoughts in the world from other people just like them. Just like trying to put the negative ends of the battery together, no matter how hard you try, your dominating thoughts will give you exactly what you are asking for. It isn't so hard to see then why a person who wants more money or wants a girlfriend or boyfriend continues to struggle. They are not thinking of the feeling they would have if they already had what they wanted. They are thinking of the LACK of what they are wanting and by law, they are getting exactly what their dominating thoughts are putting out there.

Just think of it this way and you will really want to learn *The Thinking Cure*! If you are angry, you get more anger. If you are jealous you get more jealousy. If you are full of greed and contempt, then you just get more of it. If you are full of love, kindness, generosity and compassion then you will be flooded with those same emotions from the outside world. In the book *Power vs. Force* this concept never became clearer to me. So, if there are millions of angry people and you are one of them, how do I shift from being angry to compassionate? That is what *The Thinking Cure* is all about. A very effective solution that is driven by common sense! Most people are simply never AWARE that their current thoughts are the reason they can't get the things they want or become the person they want to be. How many times have you heard people say or even said yourself, "It's just going to be a bad day." Your dominating thoughts will deliver! That is the promise of the law of attraction. Unfortunately the human species as a whole does not understand how powerful our thoughts are yet. We can see things with our eyes so we believe them. We hear things with our ears so we believe those sounds. Why is understanding this law so difficult? Because we can't see our thoughts? You can't see radio waves or cell phone waves either, but those are things we use every day and give little if NO thought to how they work. I can be in Washington DC and call someone in California and within SECONDS I am talking to them. How does that work? The guided missile part of this book is much like a radio station. You simply need to dial into the radio station of life you want. If you had a cell phone that you could just put FEEL GOOD today on your speed dial, wouldn't you call it all of the time! Your mind has that ability. *The Thinking Cure* will help you understand this.

I know, I know. "But Dave you say, you don't know my life…you don't know me…what I go through or what I've been through." I'm here to tell you it doesn't matter! My parents divorced. I've been broke. I've gone through bankruptcy. I've had cars repossessed. I've lost businesses. I have also had my youngest brother and very best friend take his own life. Yes, my brother committed suicide. I've also got married, had three incredible kids, have built three different multi-million dollar businesses, have given to my favorite charities, helped friends, visited different countries, have gone on dozens of vacations, have overcome a very shy personality and so much more. That is what Mindweaving and accomplishing goals can do for you. It can give you your life back and you can experience everything you have ever wanted.

    I don't care what you have been through. It's time to wake up and get out of that robot minded stage you are in. Stop letting society, the media, your past and the people around you run your life. Stop letting what they taught you in school keep holding you back. The status quo and the norm in the world is for everyone else. This is about YOU. Mindweaving will give you a formula, a recipe, if you will, to success, happiness and more importantly feeling good all of the time. Don't be turned off by the simplicity of this formula…all you have to know is that it works. It always works without question. You just have to know what it is and how to tap into it. They did not teach you in school. They did not teach you in church. Unfortunately, so far, not many have ever learned this. But the ones who have will attest to how effective it is. Mindweaving will have you thinking, "Maybe they will teach this to kids someday. It sure would eliminate a lot of heartaches and challenges."

    I'm glad you are taking the journey with Mindweaving. It will make your good thoughts stronger and help eliminate the bad thoughts. Making you literally a magnet for success and feeling good. I like to jump around and share some real life stories and then make a point that made dramatic impact on my life, so bear with me! I think many of you will be thinking of your own stories as I share a few of mine. I promise I won't leave you without a solution though. Let's get started!

Trim the Fat

    Most of us have heard of the Law of Attraction, the concept that made *The Secret* so popular. Unfortunately, in my opinion, they missed a huge step in that fantastic concept. Action! Yes, you actually need to do something! You also have to make your good thoughts towards the things you want to be, do or have become a habit. We spend a lot of time thinking and listening to the chatter in our heads, but we need to DO something about it.

Think of a body builder or a runner or any other athlete. What do they focus on? Why are they so physically superior than everyone else? Yes. They WORK on it. They work on their body and for the most part treat it like a temple. How many times have we purchased gym memberships or exercise equipment with the right intention, but then no action. No follow through. It happens more than it doesn't happen.

When a person works out they are trimming the fat off of their body. They are getting rid of the toxins in that fat so they have more energy and FEEL better. When was the last time you trimmed the fat off of your mind! Did you know we have over 80,000 thoughts a day, 400 billion bits of information and most of the time we don't even know what most of them are? It's time to trim the fat. How many of you have ever watched a movie and caught yourself believing that it was real? It's a movie. It's not real. Sorry. But we THINK it is. Unfortunately most people in the world ONLY LET OUTSIDE INFLUENCES like the news, a movie, a friend, a newspaper, a rumor or some other form of society decide what we think. When was the last time YOU thought for yourself! When I say think for yourself, I mean positive uplifting thoughts like the day you first rode the bike, or got an A on a test. Thinking for yourself should always be in an uplifting manner. THAT IS NOT WHAT WE ARE TAUGHT TO DO.

Mindweaving is about giving your mind a workout each day. Five to ten minutes a day will make the biggest difference in how you think. What is the old Bowflex slogan, "Give us 20 minutes a day for a rock hard body." It's time to start to treat our minds and brains just like our bodies. I heard a profound statement many years ago by one of the greatest philosophers of my time, Jim Rohn. He said, "Most people simply don't do well because they don't feel well." Guess what, it doesn't start in your body, it starts in your mind. I'll say this 100 times in this book. Feeling good is the most important thing you can do every minute of your life.

Moments that can Define your Life

It was summer of 2000. My little brother who was 26 at the time had been missing for a couple days. Not terribly unusual as he liked to have fun and party and be his own free spirit. My brother was one of my closest and best friends. We were four years apart so we grew up doing everything together. I was his big brother and I liked that responsibility. My parents divorced when he was 13 and I was 17, a tough time in a kid's life anyway. I called my mom who at the time lived in Maryland and told her it had been a couple days since we had seen him and she decided to fly home. I was driving down I70 interstate to pick her up at the airport when I got a phone call. It was my dad. He always called me Pitty. He was crying uncontrollably. I said, "Dad, what's wrong, settle down, I'm on my way to get Mom." I'll never forget the mile marker I was at and that moment in my life. My dad said the sheriff's department had found my brother. For a split second I was relieved. Then he said the unthinkable. "Pitty, they found his body in a car. He shot himself. Your little brother is dead. He killed himself."

Anyone reading this has had those moments that can certainly define you as a person. I still had 200 miles to drive alone to meet my mom at the airport. I spent the next three hours trying to figure out how to meet her at the airline gate and let her know that one of her two sons had just committed suicide, and a very brutal and graphic one at that. I spent the next year trying to figure out why a big brother would let this happen. I blamed myself, I blamed my mom, I blamed my dad…I pretty much blamed anyone that I thought of. I met mom at the gate, told her, we dropped to the ground and cried for some time. It was one of the most uneasiest and scariest times in my life. Luckily one of my very best friends was there with me. I don't think I could have done it without him. I was married with three kids and simply had to find a way to hold it together. I didn't do a very good job. I only wish I would have known then what I know now.

Friends, that is why I'm so passionate about Mindweaving and *The Thinking Cure*. I suffered for years. I went to counselors, a few psychiatrists and a plethora of people who said they could help me with this so called depression I was labeled with. They even prescribed me some great DRUGS that were supposed to help me! Did you know that the number one side effect of depression drugs is thoughts of suicide? Unbelievable. Guess what. I was not depressed. I had a little fat that had accumulated on my mind and I needed to simply trim it off. I'm here today and can honestly say 100 percent that although I still miss my brother, I feel very good about the entire experience. The event doesn't go away. BUT HOW YOU THINK ABOUT IT CAN! I have been through a bankruptcy in a town of 2500 people at the age of 25. I have watched my dad practically kill himself drinking. I have had close friends die. I have flunked tests, dropped out of college, had cars repossessed, been taken to jail, got a dozen speeding tickets and so much more! It's called life. It is a shame how we try to keep kids these days in such a small box. With so many laws, rules and things that WE, society, think is best for them. Living life is what is best for everyone. You are not going to get rid of the negative things that happen, but you can certainly think about them in a way that continues to move you forward towards your goals! It has been proven in quantum physics that when you have poor emotions they create proteins on your brain that then attract more of the same feelings. Some people are simply addicted to feeling bad and being depressed! Your brain creates certain proteins in the brain when you think this way! Watch the movie, "What the Bleep do we Know?" It is good documentary movie that shows what happens when you think a thought.

I only share these stories as each of you has the same stories. Maybe you do not have the same event, but the same emotions that have put a little fat on your brain. It's time to trim it away. That is what the exercises in this book will do. Mindweaving is my life's passion. If one person reads this book, comes to a seminar or listens to the audios and DVDs on Mindweaving and gets their thoughts back and can start to feel good all of the time, the thoughts that make you feel like you just conquered the world every day, then my goal is met. Mindweaving works. It works no differently than working out will get the fat off your body and make you physically feel better.

How to Use this Book

I've never considered myself a teacher, but a student first. I'm still learning today and I crave learning and setting new goals each and every day. When Mindweaving and *The Thinking Cure* were first thought of, it was created to help people set goals, feel good every day and accomplish everything they want in their lives. It has grown to much more than just this book. We have been overwhelmed with how much other people are craving this information, they just didn't know where to look. I was 22 years old and had a one year old and a two year old. My wife and I were entrepreneurs from the beginning and we had several businesses we were trying to run. Never in my 22 years did someone mention to me about the law of attraction, the concepts in *Think and Grow Rich*, that there was a new age section in the library that would really make me think. Never did anyone teach or tell me that I could set my own goals and I had everything I needed to achieve them inside. My best friend walked in one day and handed me a set of cassette tapes from Jim Rohn titled *The Art of Exceptional Living*. I plugged them in and I've been hooked for over 20 years. Why are we not taught and exposed to these things in school or when growing up? I am still asking myself that today as I have a thousand times.

I want you to get the most out of this book. I want you to understand the simplicity of Mindweaving and *The Thinking Cure*. The best way to do this is to just read the book all the way through. It is not a long book and it can be read cover to cover very fast. We want to ignite a spark inside of you. There is so much more at www.mindweaving.com and www.thethinkingcure.com to help not only you, but to also assist you in sharing this information with as many people that you want. This book really gives you a four step exercise that will change the way you think about your goals and how you live.

If you are like me, when I'm reading a book I hate to stop and do the exercises! So, if you are like me, then read the book all the way through, and just mark the pages with exercises. I do encourage you to take a quick mental break at each exercise and just give each one ten seconds. They are recapped several times. I want to tell you that I have applied the information in this book for the last twenty years in my life. When I do

I get the results I want; when I don't I have struggled. My struggles have simply shown me as much about the law of attraction and how mindweaving works as much as my successes have. I hope you get the same feelings. I hope you find in *The Thinking Cure* that you can eliminate the negative programs that you, with help from society have running in your mind within minutes. Imagine, a lifetime of "I can't do that," or "Who do I think I am," or "I'm so embarrassed or afraid," all gone within minutes so you can get on with what you are supposed to do. Create and feel good!

I encourage you to go to the website and sign up for our newsletters and other things. There is some great information at your fingertips on the websites and some fantastic videos of the success principles in this book. There is a Mindweaving Home Study 21 Day Boot Camp that will change your thinking habits. Share this with your friends, family, co-workers and business associates. When you, your family or team are on the same page with this information, you will accomplish so much more. You will truly have an advantage as you will soon understand after you get started reading. Our Mindweaving seminars can also be tailored to fit your specific group or company to really tie together and ignite the goals within a team or group. I will speak for everyone at Mindweavers and *The Thinking Cure*…we are excited for your journey!

Chapter 2

Your Guided Missile

One of the first books I ever truly read and applied in my life was *Psycho-Cybernetics* by Maxwell Maltz. It is still one of my favorites. It was the first time that I really believed that I could be in control of myself and my life. I was nineteen when I read that book. I just didn't know how to apply the things I was reading! They made sense. The book talked about an internal guided missile we all have. It said that squirrels have a guided missile. We all know that they gather nuts in the summer and fall getting ready for winter. No one has to teach them this. There is no squirrel school. They just do it. A squirrel's guided missile is simply set to GATHER NUTS. It is how their minds have been woven. They know exactly what to do.

We have that same internal guided missile system. If you ever watched old cartoons like Tom and Jerry they show the guided missile. Tom the cat dials the missile to say mouse. And the rest of the cartoon the missile gets changed to different settings and it simply follows what it is set to. It sounds ridiculous, but we are very much the same.

Here is a major point. Human beings have the ability to choose what their guided missile is set on…squirrels don't. Unfortunately, most human beings never choose. They simply go through life letting what their teacher said, their parents said, what the news said, their friends' opinions, their bosses' opinions and rules and so much more run their life. Very few people have a string of thoughts that are actually of their own making! That is what mindweaving is about. Getting you to own your thoughts so you can start to feel good all of the time!! Yes, it is that easy.

When I was in high school I took the SAT test that decides how smart you are and what you are going to be the rest of your life. Well, I didn't do very well in the English department. I wanted to go to a four year college and major in veterinary medicine. That was my goal. The test and the counselors suggested I go to a two year college and try to warm up and get ready for a four year college. I arrived at the two year college and they told me there that English Comp 1 would be way too hard for me, that I should take a remedial college reading and English course first. Okay, so where do you think my guided missile is at this point. I guess I'm no good at English and I'll never be able to do the things I want as these so called experts just told me so. I'm eighteen years old at the time.

I only went to school for 18 months and decided I'd rather just work. So I did. I then fell in love, got married and had my first baby girl. I then decided I better go back to school so I could support my new family! While working full time I also took, believe it or not, English Comp 2 so I could get the credits I needed to graduate. I commuted to a junior college to get this done. I was in class for about a month and actually enjoyed it. I was getting this English deal and I liked to write. Then came along our first major writing assignment, which I worked day and night on. I was extremely excited and proud when I handed this paper in as I knew how much effort and thought had gone into it. I was sitting in a class of about 45 people when the graded papers were handed back out…there was a huge F right on the top of my paper. I was crushed to say the least. Once again assuring me that I would never accomplish the things I want as I was stupid. I guess I should just settle for whatever I can do and stop trying, which is exactly what I did. I walked out of that classroom that day and never returned to school. I took the opinion of a teacher and let her put a little fat on my mind. And I carried that with me everywhere I went. I started to be afraid to talk to people as I knew my English and grammar must be horrible. I stopped thinking of what I wanted to accomplish and just started to settle for whatever came along. I never remembered being shy, but all of a sudden I had a difficult time looking at people in the eyes and being up front and genuine. Even when I was doing well in our business, I still had a hard time meeting people in a crowd and visiting. Many people who knew me in our businesses back in the mid nineties would say, "Dave was a very shy person, he would hardly even look someone in the eye." I don't know when or who started that program running in my head, but I'm certainly glad I learned *The Thinking Cure* and resolved that.

How many of us do that every day of our lives. You have an internal guided missile. I doubt right now it is set on what YOU want to do. It is probably dialed into what your boss wants, or what your parents want, or what society wants or what the normal status quo is supposed to be at the time. That is what mindweaving is going to do for you. You are going to get dialed in. We are not only going to dial in what you really want, but give you the action steps that *The Secret* and the Law of Attraction simply don't tell you.

I will say that today, I still know that English teacher and I am a much happier person. I know I flunked the class by her standards. But I also know that if that experience would not have happened, I would have probably not shocked myself into doing something I really wanted to do. Even though my grammar and English are remedial by the SAT and my teacher's standards, I have written books, spoken on hundreds of stages, recorded excellent training DVDs and have truly found a passion that makes me jump out of bed every day. Do you have a little fat that needs trimmed off of your mind like my English experience? Then let's get to it. The rest of this book is going to give you a few exercises in each chapter. Don't worry, they take five minutes and they are fun… because it finds the real you. That internal feeling of riding that bike for the first time. That feeling inside that knows you are the creator of your life and no one else. We just have to trim all the fat off that you have let society and outside influences put on there.

Guided Missile versus SONAR

I love to fish. Some of the best memories I have are at a lake just thirty minutes from my back door. I actually bought a little cabin out there I like it so much. When I first started fishing at the lake I had a mentor. Ron was the guy that everyone in town talked to when it came to fishing. When are the fish biting, what are they biting on, what time of day is best…Ron is the ultimate expert when it comes to fishing. My dad and Ron are great friends so I kind of had an in with the fishing guru in town. He first started teaching me how to fish the lake for walleye about eight years ago. We would go out on this giant body of water and he would go straight to a spot and we would start catching fish. It was amazing. We would get back to the dock and load the boat and he would ask others on the dock, "How's it going? Did you do any good?" Most of them always said no and said the fish weren't biting today. It was funny because we had our limit most of the time. They all had fancy SONAR depth finding machines on their boats better known as fish finders. SONAR works by sending a vibration down to the bottom of the lake and then bouncing back the images down there on a screen. So it is giving you a view of reality at the bottom of the lake which you can't see. It tells you where the bottom of the lake is. We too had a SONAR depth finder on our boat, but Ron always said, "That just shows you what is under the water and what depth you are at. It doesn't mean there are fish there." A big lesson I learned was this. Ron told me, "It doesn't matter if there are fish on your fish finder, you have to be fishing at the same depth that the fish are at." If the fish are at twelve feet deep and you are fishing at sixteen feet, you are not going to catch any fish. Most guys would bob around out on that water maybe fishing in the right place, just at the wrong depth. I learned all I really needed to catch all the fish I wanted is to have a good depth finder.

Your guided missile is what you dial into so you are going the direction you want to go. Your SONAR is what is bouncing back to you what is really happening. Your SONAR will tell you what depth you need to be at for achieve the things you want. How many times do people set goals, say what they want, wish it would come to them, ask and hope they receive it and pray about it. These are all fine, but if you are not thinking at the right depth, you will simply miss your goals just like you would miss the fish that are just two feet from your bait. When you start Mindweaving it is like when you first start working out and do a few push-ups or pull ups for the first time. You think, "Wow! I don't remember those being that hard!" Working on your mind when you first begin can feel the same way. *The Thinking Cure* and Mindweaving will get you to the right depth to get and become what you want. It is the same process you use to do the simple habitual things you do every day.

First we will get you dialed in to what you want…then we will make sure you are at the right depth! Most people simply do not know or do this step when it comes to the things you want. The simple act of getting in your car, starting it and driving to the grocery store is exactly how you want to approach the things you want and who you want to be. Once you understand *The Thinking Cure* and Mindweaving you will wonder, "Why in the world aren't they teaching this stuff to kids!" No one knows this stuff!

The Ten Second Wonder

If you are reading this book you have probably heard of setting goals. This is not something that I was taught in school. I have not visited with anyone in my travels that have ever shared that this is something that was taught. Maybe talked about, but not taught. Setting goals is bigger than just saying I want a new car or I want a better job. There are specific actions that will get your mind going in the same direction about your goals as it does when you are ready to eat. You have an internal guided missile system that tells you when you are hungry, when to sleep, when to be afraid and run and other spontaneous actions that require no immediate thought. In the book *The Secret* they talked so much of the Law of Attraction. I enjoyed that book and DVD and love the Law of Attraction concept. What the number one complaint seems to be from that concept is that it just didn't work for me. Well, if you only read the book, no, it probably didn't work for you.

It's like me in college wanting to be a veterinarian. I thought about it but never really applied the action steps of Mindweaving. When the action steps are applied it is like you have just rewritten a program on the computer in your brain. When you watch a movie you know it's a movie. You may be scared or sad during the movie, but when you leave you are back to reality. That is exactly how most people set goals. They last only as long as the movie lasts and the movie is your conscious thoughts. Mindweaving actually helps you write your goals and dreams on your mind. If I had applied these actions in college then I would today be a veterinarian. It's just that simple.

Have you ever been in love? So much that is hurts. All you can think about is who you are in love with, how there is no way you can be without this person. Imagine if you had goals that were that powerful in your life. Goals that defined you and made you so happy and you wanted them worse than any kind of love imaginable. Goals that will have you ready to climb a mountain or blow the darn thing up to get to where you are going. Do you have goals like that in your life? The processes in this book will help you do that. I have applied these time and time again in my life. This book is not about me, but my successes were achieved by applying these applications.

I grew up in a small central Kansas farm town and did not finish college. I have experienced a bankruptcy, quitting college, my parents divorced, my brother committed suicide, by businesses had failed and so on and so on. It's like a broken record of most people's lives. I then was introduced to this concept of goal setting. Even though setting goals is good, they are only empty wishes unless you can apply action to them so they are as real as eating dinner tonight is. That is the magic. That is the ten second wonder. Get your goals so vivid that all you have to do is think about them for ten seconds and your mind is going in the proper direction. Also, when you are in this state of mind, the outside sources and influences do not bother you. The old saying, "You have to stand for something or you will fall for anything," is a bit true. Most people fall for whatever they hear next. When you are focused and dialed in and you know what you want as much as you know the sun is coming up tomorrow…you are on your way. It is not a hard principle to understand and it is the easiest and funnest exercise and action you will ever do. It is you!! It is the real internal guidance system that is hidden deep inside you wanting to erupt like a volcano and give you everything you want!

Major point: It is the easy success principles and the easy things in life that are also easy not to do.

I heard a statement a long time ago that said, "You become what you think about most of the time." Some of you may recognize it from Earl Nightingale's famous speech, The Strangest Secret. You become what you think about most of the time. Guess what you and your subconscious think about most of the time? You got it. Crap! A typical day for someone is to wake up and go to a job they don't like. Live with someone they don't really like. They listen to everyone else who has the same crappy lives and jobs they don't like. They then turn on the news or sit down after work and watch four hours of TV and let the media determine what is real in their life. I could go on and on. We actually will watch TV drug commercials that tell us that we could develop cancer, blindness, thoughts of suicide and even die from taking them…they are the biggest companies in the world. We are that desperate to FEEL GOOD!

It is time to get dialed in. It is time to activate Your Guided Missile. It's time to set some goals and put action to them so you are thinking about them even when you are sleeping. It's time to write the things and events that you want to happen in your life in a way that you get them. Period. I have gone from being labeled reading and writing handicapped to becoming the top business and sales leader in several different companies. After creating millions and millions of dollars in those businesses, I walked away from them to start all over and start my own business. I applied these techniques and once again, I had a multi-million dollar business in less than six months. I've applied these in my relationships, in how I raise my kids and how I live my everyday life. Does it mean I'm perfect…no way. But I do know how to set goals in a way that I'm literally attracted to the right things. I have traveled to different countries, been on cruises, driven luxury vehicles, given away more money in a month than I used to make and so much more. Remember, you become what you think about most of the time. What are you thinking about right now? How about right before you picked the book up? How about right when you go to sleep? When I learned this and believed it, I started thinking about only the things that would help me win and feel good all of the time.

We simply have not been taught or ever learned either how powerful our internal guided missile is or how to engage it. That is what Mindweaving and the rest of this book is going to do.

Past Experiences

Think of a past experience? What did you think of? Ninety-five percent of the people I ask this to live or in coaching think of something bad. It is crazy but true. Let's change the way we think right here. This is a vital and powerful step in Mindweaving.

Now think of a past experience that you were so proud in. An experience that made you feel amazing. Think of a good past experience. We will tie all this together later, but this is a powerful exercise. And IT WILL MAKE YOU FEEL GOOD. Remember, feeling good every minute of every day is the ultimate goal.

I think about my kids a lot when I do this exercise. I can remember the day each one of my kids was born. I can almost smell the hospital it's so vivid. My wife had C sections on all three and I was the first one to get to hold each one of my kids…I'm selfish like that! I remember them looking up at me, grabbing my finger with their hand, giving me total control over them and trusting me 100 percent with their lives. I think about going fishing. I love fishing. There have been times where I have been nervous or in a situation I did not want to be in and I simply start to think about fishing for walleye on a lake just a few miles from where I live. It is heaven. I remember one specifically when the weather and wind was so bad that no one should have been on the lake. I had taken my dad fishing that day and we were about to call it quits as the wind was actually bringing water over the boat and our trolling motor had actually broke off in the waves! But we started catching fish. My wife has told me repeatedly that when the dream is big enough THE FACTS DON'T COUNT! We were about to drown the boat but we not only started catching fish, we caught more large walleye in the next 45 minutes than either of us ever had before. It was one of the greatest experiences ever for me and my dad was with me.

I think of the day I got married…looking at my amazing red headed wife and knowing I could spend the rest of my life with my best friend. Both of our parents were divorced and it was one of the only times our entire families were ever together. My wedding day was one of the best experiences I have of my brother, Scott, as well. He was so proud of me and loved my wife as much as me. I remember the wedding day ending and going to our suite and just relaxing and relishing in that moment, "we just got married." I remember the day I got my first car. It was a 1976 purple Camaro. It needed a lot of work but it was mine! My dad went to a body shop and bought me a pile of wet sand paper. He said, "If you want this car painted then you have to sand all of the purple paint off of it." I spent hundreds of hours sanding that car down by hand. I remember the day it came rolling out of the body shop with a fresh coat of metallic dark blue paint. I can still smell it. I felt so free, so grown up, so much responsibility. I remember the first time someone asked me to speak on stage in front of a crowd. It was the most nervous I've ever been! But it was the most rewarding feeling afterwards when people started telling me I made a difference in their life.

We all have experiences that are great. Experiences that make us FEEL GOOD. Isn't it funny that sometimes the only time we think about them is when we sit around with friends and are just reminiscing. Listen sometimes to guys in their 30s and 40s talk about back in the day when they were in high school and that winning football team. When you are listening it is like you are sitting right there in the crowd!

I know I know, we all have bad experiences too. How do I not always let them creep in my mind and only think of the good things. Hang on! We are getting there, this is a process! There is quite a bit of fat to trim off of some of our minds! If you want to think of this process in its simplest terms think about this. When you sit down to eat pizza you have eaten pizza before. You know you like pizza so it is not that big of a deal, you may actually be craving the pizza because you have been THINKING about it for awhile. Each meal you eat that you thoroughly enjoy you actually thought about before you put it in your mouth, even if subconsciously. If not you would always be apprehensive to put anything in your mouth. You know what you like when it comes to food. It's time to start knowing what you like in life. It's like a huge buffet since we are talking about food. You walk up and down the buffet putting the things you like on your plate. What would happen if someone came up and started putting things on your plate you didn't like! You would be like, "Hey! Stop that, I don't like beets!" Have you ever wondered why you are letting people put those same things you don't like on your mind? Driving your car is the same process. You have had a good experience driving your car as it got you to where you needed to go. The next time you get in your car you have no problem starting your car, putting it in gear and going. Imagine doing that at the age of seven years old? You would be scared to death, not sure what to do and worried about the experience. With a few good experiences you now don't even think about it, your guided missile is on auto pilot when it comes to driving. What happens when someone has a wreck and has a bad experience? Usually nothing.

This is a powerful point. Even if you crash your car, you can still get in it the next day and drive it like any other day. It's like when you finally learn to ride that bike without training wheels. The goal and FEELING of riding that bike with no training wheels will let you crash a few times, get hurt, and get back on! When you have had a good experience in something your subconscious will draw from that experience. I know eating pizza, walking through a buffet and driving a car are pretty simple things, but there was a day you could not do any of them, now you could do them very easily. Remember earlier when I said some people are addicted to feeling bad and feeling depressed. Well you can be addicted to feeling good just the same way. IT IS A DECISION. YOURS!

There are so many things we take for granted in our lives such as eating, driving, walking, talking, shaving, how to tie your shoes and so many more. We did not learn these things without having a few good experiences. Likewise, we did not just quit these things when we had a bad experience. Once your guided missile is dialed in, the bad experiences are just learning experiences. You can live your life and set goals to be, do or have anything you want no different than you learned to walk. Most of us though take things so personally and seriously in life that we let one bad experience completely stop us from pursuing our goals. Mindweaving is going to help you learn how to accomplish anything you want in your life. It is going to teach you how to use great past experiences to ignite future goals. In all my successes and material things in my life, knowing how to control my thinking to benefit me and accomplish everything I want to be, do or have is the most valued thing sitting on my shelf.

EXERCISE

I want you to get a blank notebook or eventually get one of the Mindweaving Daily journals from the website. I want you write down five good experiences in your life. Not things that are going to happen. These are things prior to right now. The first time I rode a bike. The first time I kissed a girl/boy. The first time I drove. The day I got married. The day I had my first child. I just want you to list them and not be really in depth yet. Usually out of bad experiences come great experiences. Few people would ever say their parent's divorcing is a good thing. I didn't like it. I remember, though, standing at the bottom of our stairs in our house. My dad had left and my mom was struggling. I looked at her and asked if she was going to be okay. She looked back at me as deeply as she ever has and said, "If you are going to be okay then I will be okay." I knew then we would all be just fine. I remember in one of my businesses our guy in charge of finances was not paying the bills for shipping. We owed over $50,000 to Fed Ex for our open account. What a terrible thing, right? Well, another guy that worked for me took this task to heart and started researching better ways to ship products. We got hooked up with the post office and a program that literally saved us over $250,000 in shipping products in the next eighteen months. Sometimes you can really find some good out of something you once thought was so bad.

Now I want you to get the note book and actually write out those experiences. If you are like most people something dramatic will happen to you. The more you do this the more your mind will constantly shift to good things in your life. You also start to attract only good things and good experiences. Why? Because we become what we think about most of the time! Take some time to either write or type these out so you really remember them. They are your experiences so remembering them is easy, but I want you to get detailed in your thoughts. If it is a college graduation that is one of your experiences, what were you wearing, was it cold outside or warm outside, who was there to watch you, what did you go through to get that degree. If it the first time you drove what color was the car? How did you feel? What did you think? Take some time to do this exercise; we will use it later and magical things will happen.

Here is a good example of G.E.T (great experience thoughts). I remember the day my youngest daughter, Kali Anne, was born. I actually remember my kids being born like it was yesterday. I relive the days. But on the day my youngest daughter was born it was so amazing because my other two kids were there! Brooklyn was almost five and Chance was three years old and they were bringing home baby sister Kali. I can still see the looks on their faces. I have pictures of Brooklyn and Chance with this little new sister Kali with the biggest smiles on their faces that I've ever seen. I still see them caring for this little thing like it was a new little kitten or something we brought home. I remember what friends came to the hospital and what the weather was like when I loaded my wife up to bring them all home. Knowing that I had a part in creating these experiences is amazing. Don't let the big things in your life become little insignificant things just because you stop thinking about them.

If you are sitting around with a friend, or family member or say, "Do you remember when?" Mention the time a child was born, or someone won a special award. Listen to them talk…it is like it happened yesterday. That is going back in the past and finding a great experience that you can draw from.

Chapter 3

Defining Your Dreams and Goals

What you will start to realize is that you will finally have a proven method for actually setting goals and achieving them instead of just pie in the sky wishes. You are a creator. You have an internal guided missile inside you and one of two things is going to happen.

1. You will be like a ship without a rudder and aimlessly cruise around the bay with no idea what wind will take your sail to the next place.

2. You will define the things you want most in your life and have a simple process for achieving them.

This isn't just a goal setting 101 class. This is how to put the law of attraction to work for you with action. You are already a magnet attracting everything that you have in your life now… if you want different things, then think differently. Remember, you become what you think about most of the time.

In the next few chapters we will talk about an exercise that actually has you tell yourself WHY you want the things you do. So many don't know what they want…they just know what they don't want. I don't want to be broke which means I want more money. I don't want to be lonely so I want a partner. I don't want this piece of junk car, I want one that runs. Mindweaving will help you find the reasons that actually either make you broke or give you more money. You get to choose which way you want it. This is the big issue with the law of attraction. If I know I'm broke and I need more money and that is where I leave it…then what is the law of attraction going to give me? The feeling of being broke and the fact I know I need more money. It is the silliest thing when you really think about it and it really clears up why you are the way you are!

Let's talk about goals for a little. This is an important subject and is really what the ten second miracle is all about. You have to know what to put on your guided missile and what to dial it into! Again, most people NEVER do this. They simply let the winds determine the set of their sail. Let's change that. Let's let our internal system do what is was designed to do and that is to create and make us feel good! Believe it or not, feeling bad is just as much of a choice as feeling good. Here is a key statement to keep close to you. This statement will help you understand why you always stay where you are and struggle instead of feel amazing, full of energy and getting the things you want.

Most people are either afraid of the future or ashamed of the past. Rarely are you living in the right now. Right now is your launching pad for creating. Right now is what your next five minutes are being built in. Most people live being ashamed of the past or afraid of the future AND THAT IS WHAT YOU BASE YOUR LIVING IN THE NOW ON. That is why it is so easy to listen to what others say and take it as law, because you can't make a decision for yourself! I've never seen a group of people in society struggle and suffer more from this concept than teenagers. I feel so sorry for them and wish so badly they knew this information. Some of the most brutal and emotional times in a person's life are those teenager years. Things happen with friends and school that keep you afraid of tomorrow and ashamed of what just happened.

Being dialed into your guided missile and defining your goals will help you live in the right now! Imagine going to a restaurant as you are starving. This particular restaurant is a huge buffet. If it weren't for your guided missile, you may start putting things on your plate that you don't like. You are not afraid of the past when it comes to food you

Defining Your Dreams and Goals

don't like, you are dialed into what you do like. Likewise, if there are things on the buffet that look good but you have never tried them, you know it is okay to throw them away if you don't like the taste. When it comes to decisions in your life you can have the same attitude towards everything in the past and future. The only reason you let the past affect you is because you are not dialed into your guided missile and you do not have a defined goal you are shooting for. Something that makes you jump out of bed in the morning. Same is true with the future. If you are afraid of the future then you are apprehensive because you are not dialed into the now and fired up about living. Worse yet, you never move forward in your life because you are comparing what happened in the past! Mindweaving will help you tremendously start living in the now and knowing exactly where you are headed.

So let's get to work and start to define what you really want. This exercise may seem like overkill, but once we tie everything together, Mindweaving will show you a fifteen minute exercise that brings this entire book together. I want you to take a clean white sheet of paper and if you have a pen with blue ink that is best. I want you to write at the top of the page, "My wildest dreams and goals." I want you to start making a list of things that you would do, have or be if money and time were no object. No judging allowed! Just let yourself flow with big things as well as small things. Maybe you want to go out to eat more often, possibly a new car, a new place to live. How about simple things like paying off some lingering bills, a new pair of shoes, or a nice watch. How about a trip you have always wanted to go on. Maybe you see people struggle and would like to help them by giving to charities or more to your church. Maybe you want to build a church. Maybe you are wanting to go college and become a teacher or doctor. Take some time and just make a good list. If you are married it might not hurt to do this with your partner and family. Make it fun! No judging. Just let the creative side of you bubble up the things that you have be, do or have if money and time was not an issue. Are you a shy person and you want to be out going? Are you single and you want a fun friend or partner? Get personal about these goals! Sometimes we think of setting goals with only material things. You can define who YOU are in your goal setting and Mindweaving.

I remember doing this exercise for the first time when I was 26 years old. I thought to myself, "How goofy is this!" I'm in the middle of a bankruptcy, I'm working as many hours as humanly possible, I have two kids and a third one on the way and I just didn't think I had the time to write down a bunch of pie in the sky goals and dreams. This was one of the most important exercises I ever did. In the months and years to come…every single goal that was on my sheet of "Dave's Wildest Dreams and Goals" had been accomplished. Mindweaving is one of those things that will have you thinking…can it really be this simple? Is this really how my mind works and why I get and have the things I do? And the answer is yes, it is. Remember, you become what you think about most of the time. MOST PEOPLE NEVER THINK ABOUT THE THINGS THEY WANT! They are always thinking of what they are lacking! If they do they are afraid of the future or ashamed of the past and the thought passes quickly. There is no ACTION applied to lock in the goal and actually write a new program on your brain! Most people think about what they want as a wondering thought. Mindweaving will write it on your subconscious and get rid of the old bad programming.

Next I want you to take another clean sheet of paper and write down these things again but this time be specific. Take a little time and clarify each of your wildest goals. If you wrote down a new car. This time write, "I want a brand new black on black Mercedes 550. I want the one with the leather interior and the wood trim…." Be specific. If you are wanting to help a specific group or charity, which one? Get your creative mind not just creating, but creating things that are emotional for you! I remember one of my goals was to become a speaker that made an impact on people's lives. I set this goal after the first time I was ever asked to give a speech on success. I was very shy at the time so this was a huge step for me. Answer these questions.

Who would you like to be?
What would you like to have?
What would you like to do?

One huge lesson I learned was when I read Psycho-Cybernetics back in 1989. One of the first chapters talked about a person's imagination. YOUR MIND DOES NOT KNOW THE DIFFERENCE BETWEEN WHAT IS REAL AND WHAT IS IMAGINED. The more detailed you imagine something, the more real it is to your mind, which means it even is thinking about it when YOU are not! Isn't it interesting as a child how easy and fun it was to use our imaginations. You could fly, you could sing, you could be the president, you could be a doctor, you could be anything you wanted to be and BELIEVED you were that person! You imagined it. As adults we think or are taught that imagination is just pie in the sky stuff, it's time to get to work. Unfortunately if we just would have kept on imagining and not letting the outside world influence us we would have became all we wanted to be.

Imagination is powerful and your mind does not know what is real or what is imagined. This sentence changed my life. I have heard this statement from at least fifteen other authors and speakers.

This step is very powerful and starts the process that makes you physically excited about what you are doing. Most people think of what they want to do, be or have and within a few minutes talk themselves right out of it. This step is a very powerful step. It will make you dream about the things you want and wake up thinking about them. Let's move on after a quick recap.

A quick recap:

We have listed some of the things in our past that have made us feel amazing and good.

We have written down our wildest list of dreams and goals.

We have then written them down again but trying to be very specific.

I want to add an important exercise in with this recap. That is to go and get pictures of the things that you want. I know this sounds different, but remember, we become what we think about most of the time and pictures are really what the ten second miracle is all about to me.

When you start these exercises it is nice to look at your mirror or notebook and see not only words but pictures of the things you want! The first time I did this I felt really goofy. I was in Chicago at a seminar. My wife and I were walking into the Rosemont Theatre and there was a Q45 Infinity in the parking lot. My wife loved this car. Granted it was a $40,000 car back in 1996. She wanted a picture and I didn't! She reminded me that this was part of the dreambuilding process so I agreed. I also agreed because I didn't argue with the red headed wife very much! I still have that picture today. I was 26 years old standing in the middle of Chicago, Illinois, in front of a black Q45 Infinity sedan with plush cream leather interior inside. It even had a little gold clock right in the middle of the dash. We did not have the money to buy this car but it was fun to dream. Well, a month later the company we were a part of launched a free car bonus program. If you did well and accomplished x,y and z you got a free car. You guessed it. Within seven months of me standing in front of that car and getting my picture taken it was sitting in my driveway. It may sound goofy, but when was the last time you went and took pictures with the things you wanted? I remember taking pictures on the stages at the meetings I attended, not because I was speaking there, but because someday I wanted to impact people just as the speakers had impacted me.

Go get pictures of the things you want. It is really powerful if you are in the picture, but just printing them off of the internet is fine too. With you in the picture your mind actually sees you having it already and it makes the next step much easier. Hang these pictures up where you can see them every day. Remember, you become what you think about. Your mind does not know the difference between what is real and imagined. With over 400 billion bits of information coming in it is going to cling to and remember what it sees the most. What pictures does your mind see right now?

Let's Roll the Movie

Now we are going to write them one more time but this time explaining why these things would make us feel so good. This is a step of dream building and goal setting that most people have never learned

Defining Your Dreams and Goals

and a step that I've only heard one other teacher teach. It is very powerful. In the best-selling book and DVD *The Secret* they focus a lot on simply thinking about what you want and asking and you shall receive, how to just think about something and the Law of Attraction will bring it to you. Unfortunately you have to apply some energy and work to that concept and most people actually think about what they don't want and attract more of that. When you "roll the movie" you are FEELING GOOD as you just played out why this specific thought makes you feel so good. How many times have you planned a vacation and it just made you excited thinking about it. You knew the vacation was coming, you knew the things you were going to see and do on the vacation, how you were going to get there, what the weather would be like and how much fun you were going to have…and you weren't even on the vacation yet! This is how you should treat your goals. DEFINE them so they become a reality. You become what you think about most of the time. Not only do most people never set goals, they never think back to great experiences in their life and 99 percent never think of a goal or dream and say to themselves, "Now why will this make me feel good?" THAT IS THE ACTION AND ENERGY BEHIND THE LAW OF ATTRACTION! It is now personal to you…you are now creating!

This also explains a lot of why athletes are so competitive and focused. They have been dialed in to a goal for so long. Not only are they dialed in, they have seen themselves in the lights, they have heard their name on the loud speaker winning. I've heard people say, "Yeah, well if I had that new car I'd have a good attitude too." Newsflash, it is not the car that gives you the feeling, it is the feeling that gives you the car. Read this about ten times and let this sink in. This is the secret if there ever has been one. It is not the "thing or experience" that gives you the feeling… it is the "feeling" that gives you the thing or the experience. Imagine if you had been taught this from about five years old on.

Take your list of specific goals and dreams and after each one write a reason or two of why this will make you FEEL GOOD. A new car would make me feel good because…

I would like to give $10,000 to xyz charity because…

I want to go out to eat more often because…
I would like to move into a new home because…

Sometimes an amazing thing happens. There are things you thought you wanted and when you try to tell yourself why it would make you feel good, there are no reasons. Guess what? You don't really want that! It's just a wish. You need to get more specific about that goal and then go back and say, okay, NOW why would that make me feel good. This is an exercise that you should get into the habit of doing every time you look at something or think of something you think you really want. Simply say, "Now why would that make me feel good?" Try it now! The more specific you can be about the things you want or the person you want to become, the more reasons you will have of why it will make you feel so good. Feeling good is the number one goal of all human beings 100 percent of the time. Most people use the Law of Attraction against themselves! They think of a goal or something they want and immediately tell themselves why it can't happen. Then the Law of Attraction works perfectly, you don't get it as you told yourself you won't! This step of finding the good in the goals you have set for yourself is magical…and in our opinion at Mindweaving and *The Thinking Cure* the missing step and link in goal setting and goal ACHIEVING!

Chapter 4

Find the Good in Everything

I was listening to a CD one day from Jerry and Esther Hicks. They were visiting with Abraham and were talking about a subject called Pivoting. It made a big impact in my life. Sometimes it's easy to see the glass half full or to know you want something to happen, you just keep finding all the reasons why it won't. Well pivoting is essentially what we did in the last step by rolling the movie. Finding the good in everything you think about, but not just things you have or have experienced. This takes it a step further and allows your mind to know why you must have the thing you are thinking about, because you have told your mind why it WILL FEEL GOOD. A negative thought is okay, you just need to realize it as an indicator and then find the opposite of that negative, which is, why is this good?

A profound thought that was mentioned on this CD was, "Sometimes by having a negative feeling and knowing what we don't want, we then know exactly what we do want." When you are feeling negative it is because you are thinking about what you don't want. Pivot points change your energy instantly as you define the good in what you are thinking about.

Imagine if you live somewhere where it hasn't rained for a very long time. This is the example that Abraham used in the CD I listened to. It is dry and drought conditions. You go outside and think to yourself, "My goodness it's hot. I just wish it would rain. Everything is so dry, just look around. Animals have nothing to drink, it's so hot and on and on and on." So the goal is that you want it to rain. If the law of attraction works then all of your thoughts are just going to bring more of a drought. Yes, you want it to rain, but you are FOCUSED ON THE DROUGHT, THE DRY LAND AND NO WATER. The missing link in how to apply the law of attraction in your life is pivoting and finding the good in your goals. A better way to make it rain and use the Mindweaving might sound like this. "Wow, it is hot and dry. I would sure like to see some rain. When it rains it will feel so good. It will cool everything off, it will give all of the animals a nice fresh cool drink of water. The flowers, grasses and land will flourish and become so beautiful with the rain. The smell of the air changes right before a rain. The sky darkens, sometimes you can hear the thunder and actually feel the rain before it comes." Do you see the difference? Now you are attracting rain! You are applying the law of attraction and it will only respond to the good positive reasons why you want the things you want. Think of drought, and you get drought. Think of why you want it to rain and the good feeling reasons behind it, now you are attracting what you want.

When you don't have enough money and can't pay the bills how do you feel? Exactly, negative, bad, no hope, what am I going to do and a host of other negative thoughts. If you are financially challenged at the moment, then ask yourself what you would do with the money you are going to earn? What will it do for you? "I know I'm financially challenged at the moment, but oh how good it will feel when I can pay off that bill, or take my spouse out to a nice dinner, or put gas in the car to help me get around"…find the good and roll the movie. It seems simple because it is. It is just a decision. My mentor drove into my subconscious a phrase that has made me millions. SUCCESS IS A DECISION AWAY. Think about that for a minute. What thoughts are in your mind all of the time. You do have the ability to make a decision and put whatever thoughts you want up there.

It seems on the subject of money people get very touchy and really lose belief in the fact that they can have all they want. If the law of attraction is true, which it is, then we should be able to think about a thought and get it. That is what *The Secret* and the gurus tell us and that is partly true! We just have to make sure we are thinking of what we really want! Here is a scenario. I want more money, because I can't pay the bills. Everytime I sit down to pay the bills I get a gut ache. What am I going to do. I need to make more money, I need to make more money, I need to make more money…guess what? If the law of attraction is true, you will always "need to make more money." Your mind does not know what needing more money and having all the money in the world means. It doesn't care either. Its job is to give you what you are thinking about. Does that make sense? You are attracting the feeling of "needing more money." This is such a simple pivot. This is such a dramatic paradigm shift in your mind that if you learn nothing else from this book other than this you will be better. So how do you go from needing money to having money? This is the process we are going through in this entire book. Once we get to the end, we will have a concise fifteen minute method to make sure you are thinking of the things you want, as well as put action and fuel behind it so you internally believe you can actually have everything you want to be, do or have. Instead of thinking of needing money, think of the feeling when the bills are paid. If you are hungry and internally you know you are hungry then you simply get something to eat. You THINK of the food you are going to eat and it makes you FEEL GOOD. In some cases it makes your mouth water! If you stayed stuck in the thought, "I'm so hungry" and didn't have a goal to eat then you would die of starvation. You would never eat. Most people are dying of mental starvation all of their lives. The only things on their minds are the fat that someone else put there. WE SIMPLY HAVE NOT BEEN TAUGHT AS HUMAN BEINGS HOW TO ACCESS THE LAW OF ATTRACTION. Books like this are on the leading edge of teaching people how to live the happiest and most fulfilling lives. You don't have to starve, you don't have to be unhappy, you don't have to be broke. But if you constantly think of only those things, then you will get exactly that.

We can't get away from or eliminate negative feelings, we can only replace them with something better. Remember, a negative feeling is simply an internal indicator that is telling you that you are not in alignment with who you are. Negative feelings are okay, they just are telling you what you don't want so you can immediately pivot and know what you do want. That is the creation process in you. If you stay in the negative attitude, then you will certainly attract more of that. Remember, your mind does not know the difference from what is real or what is imagined. It will work towards whatever you dial into your guided missile. So why not get dialed into what you want.

Once again, I was listening to a CD by Jerry and Esther Hicks on their Art of Allowing segments with Abraham. Abraham made a very big statement that made me understand how abundant everything is that we want. He said, "When you wake up in the morning and you walk outside are you afraid that there is not enough air in the world for everyone and you just try to breathe really fast to suck it all up?" Of course not, we know there is plenty of air so by the law of attraction we have all of the air we need. We are not concerned on breathing as much as we possibly can and saving it up in fear I won't have enough air. Then why do we think of other things in our lives that way. Like money, relationships and other material things. There is an abundance of money, people, relationships, food, shelter, clothing and so many other material things that we should think of them no differently than the air we breathe. When we do that, we are creating and attracting at a super pace. Remember, we become what we think about most of the time. Think of what you want, who you want to be and where you want to be, think of abundance in these areas and you get abundance. Think of lack and you get lack. It is like gravity…it just works that way. We don't question gravity, we know if we go to the top of a building and jump, we are going down. We can't see it…we just believe it. Years from now people will have everything they have ever wanted and live the most abundantly happy lives. Someday the law of attraction will be understood the same as gravity is understood today. Many people believe that is the transition that will start to happen in 2012. Not the end of the world…but a new beginning where people don't have to live in constant suffering based on what the outside world has taught them. They will understand that they have 100 percent complete control over everything and it starts inside of them. It always has…we just stopped looking for it.

Trusting Yourself

How do we learn? As a child we are taught in a negative way. DON'T TOUCH THAT, don't do that, don't say that, stop doing that. As a child our teacher grades us and we learn by what we did wrong! We are graded and have red pen all over our tests. We are compared against the rest of the class and start to learn that I am either dumb or I struggle with this or that. Socrates was one of the greatest philosophers of all time. Back in that era a person was not allowed to question the law or what was considered right. One of the first colleges was started by Socrates and his methods. He was eventually put to death as he was teaching and questioning the way things were. Socrates is a person worth studying a bit more when you have time. It shows you in a way how the way we think has been born and bred into us.

In a way, we are brought up that way. We are to honor our elders and not question anything. Sit down and shut up. Don't speak unless spoken too. These types of thought processes shut down the creative process and most people never wake up from this type of coma. The Mindweaving process re-ignites your nerves in your brain and gets your creative process going. It allows you for maybe the first time in your life to understand why you get the things you get! You asked for them! If you are in a bad relationship I imagine you tell everyone you know about this. You think about this relationship and the challenges you are having and how you can fix it. This is what you are going to get then! A relationship that needs fixed and isn't going right. You think about it all the time so that is what you get. Remember, you become what you think about most of the time. The Mindweaving process has you thinking of what you want to be, things you want to have or do and puts action steps to them so they are written on your subconscious. Instead, go through the Mindweaving exercises and think of what a perfect relationship would be to you. What would make you feel amazing in a relationship? How would those things make you feel? There are a lot of emotions in relationships which is why you can fall madly in love one day and be wondering the next day. You have to think about what you want in a relationship and attach the great feelings to that. Your mind does not know the difference in what is real or imagined, so no differently that

The Thinking Cure

ordering your dinner off of a menu…you are ordering your life to be a certain way. It is truly that simple. Would you be confused if you were sitting at a restaurant and you had placed your order and you ordered the baked ham and when the waiter brought your dinner it was fried fish? Of course you would. Treat your life the same way. YOU GET FROM LIFE WHAT YOU ORDER AND ASK FOR…MOST PEOPLE NEVER ORDER! THEY SETTLE FOR TABLE SCRAPS.

Don Miguel Ruiz, the author of *The Four Agreements*, taught me a very valuable lesson. He said that in your mind there is a parasite. It is the judge and the victim. This judge will judge you and keep you ashamed of the past. There is also a victim, the person that is hopeless, and this victim will keep you so afraid of the future you won't do anything. The only food this parasite of the judge and victim can feed on is negative emotion. Get rid of the negative emotion and YOU RULE YOU! Mindweaving gets rid of these negative emotions by replacing them with not only positive emotions, but with the things that specifically make you feel good! Most all negative emotion is born from the outside world. Society has a place for you and you believe it. The news reports how terrible everything is and you believe it. The judge and victim eat this up and start to plant seeds of fat on your brain. Your mind just simply fills up with fat that is all negative emotion and terrible things that you hear about from friends, society, news, media, TV, radio, parents, teachers, preachers and others. They are only their opinions… but we take them so seriously we write them on our brain.

This leads us to a very powerful exercise that can eliminate and help dissolve that negative fat on our minds, getting over Hang Ups. I wanted to include this in the Mindweaving book as it can make a dramatic difference in negative experiences in your life in an instant. Remember, your mind does not know what is real or what is imagined. And we become what we think about most of the time. The law of attraction says that like attracts like. So we simply just need to think of the perfect scenario for us all of the time! Simple! Well, it is, except for the fact we are surrounded by a tremendous amount of negative and have not been taught anything in this book. We are so young as a human species. We take everything that we hear OUTSIDE of us and take it for

Find the Good in Everything

truth and rarely listen to what is INSIDE of us. Two hundred years from now people will be saying, "Can you believe they used to think that way? It must have been a living hell. I'm so glad we don't have to think that way." They will compare our way of thinking to that of how we think of the caveman. Think about it. This information is on the leading edge of thought and you have it in your hands. We will talk later about practice so you simply become a magnet for what you want to be, do or have.

I remember growing up as a young child with great loving parents, but they also ruled with an iron fist. If I back talked my mom, I knew when my dad came home I would be in their bedroom just waiting for him to come home and whip me with the belt. The fear of him coming home was worse than the actual spanking! My parents divorced when I was 17 years old. It was an odd time in my life, but I can say today that I love them both more than I ever have. My brother committed suicide ten years ago and I was so full of hatred and blame it was unbearable. I remember what my mentor had beat into my head. "Dave, Success is simply a decision away. You are deciding to feel and think this way." It made me mad, but I knew he was right. I pulled out a few books, I went through the hang up exercise I'm getting ready to share and I got my head on straight again. I had not worked for almost ten months, I was mean to my kids, I was mean to my wife. I was a wreck. I had lost my little brother and I was looking for someone to blame. I had let some fat accumulate on my brain. I felt badly and those bad proteins started accumulating, and then everything I looked at was bad. Once I started dialing back into what I needed to do, what I wanted to be and once I started to allow everyone else to just be who they are…I changed overnight. The Mindweaving process gave me my life back.

I started working again in my business and I became much more successful than ever before. We actually built two different multi-million dollar businesses AFTER all this had happened. I have an amazing love and feeling of gratitude towards my parents as I understood why they raised me the way they did. I started to overcome that bitter attitude towards life because I thought it was UNFAIR to me. Life is just life. You decide what you want out of it and what it will give to you. The next exercise saved my life so many times. I don't mean as in I was going to die or live. I mean it made me understand everyone around me, and helped me understand this powerful statement. THEY ARE ONLY OPINIONS. Just because a friend, relative, parent, teacher, priest, the news, media or anyone else says something doesn't mean it is fact…it is only an opinion. I want to talk some on this subject and Hang Ups.

Chapter 5

Hang Ups

We all know what it is like to feel good. We have discussed this and made a list of things that have made us feel amazing in our life. Mindweaving is about setting yourself up to feel that way all of the time. When you feel like that you are creating…and you are creating whatever is planted in your mind. That is how the law of attraction works. If you are full of hate, you will attract more hate. Have you ever been around someone for so long that you start to talk like them or start to have their mannerisms? That is the law of attraction. You become what you think about most of the time.

There are times in your life when things come up that may seem unbearable and extremely negative. They can be called hang ups. I've heard them called speed bumps or detours as well. I attended a leadership weekend seminar in 1995. It was in Palm Springs, California, and my friend and the greatest teacher I've ever listened to, Kevin Trudeau, was teaching the entire weekend. This subject of hang ups came up and had a big impact on my life. I have used and lived by this exercise for the past fifteen years and I know it is big part of any successful person's thinking. A few years later I was asked to go and speak to a group of people about hang ups. By teaching this to others I really learned how real hang ups are in real life. These are real life situations that have actually physically happened. If you are walking down a set of stairs and your coat or sleeve gets caught on a nail you are hung up. You are stuck and can't keep moving. This is what hang ups can do in your life. Hang Ups are not bad! They simply are bad when you stay hung up on them! Many of you know people who are sharing the same sob story for the last ten years. They just can't seem to stop talking about all of the bad things that have happened to them or other people. That is the law of attraction, like attracts like. Imagine people that gossip all of the time and then wonder why their lives are so empty. They are taking on everyone else's issues they gossip about. Imagine what the media is doing to our country and ultimately all mankind. Constant negative news is all they play. Twenty-four hours a day, seven days a week. I'm going to suggest that for twenty-one days while you are doing these exercises and getting dialed in, you unplug your TV from the wall.

Imagine being on an airplane and you are flying to do an important business meeting. You are mentally preparing on the plane and behind you is a dad and three kids. The three kids are going crazy as the plane takes off. You think no big deal, I'm sure they will settle down once we get going, they are just excited. It only gets worse. They are jumping, bouncing, banging into the back of your seat and louder than anyone else on the plane. They are eating candy and keep reaching over the seat and wiping it on your suit without any acknowledgement that you are there. You look over at the dad and he is just staring out the window and doing nothing about it! Many of us would think, "Oh my god, will this guy please take care of his kids!" Some of us might even turn around and say, "Please take care of your kids!"

This is just one example of a hang up. Something out of your control but you are in the middle of the situation. This is a hang up. Let's get rid of it in an instant. This man is just leaving his wife's funeral and these three kids just buried their mom. They are on their way home and the dad is beside himself, oblivious to his surroundings. His kids are dealing with it how kids do, they act like kids.

Do you now think a bit differently about this situation? Who cares if it is true or not? You mind does not know what is real or imagined. I want to set myself up to feel good and win all of the time. If this situation is hanging me up then I'm going to think of something to make it different and understandable. Most people try to ignore the situation, and by doing that you are just focusing on it more and you get more frustrated. Just because you put a band aid on a cut doesn't mean the cut isn't there. You need to address the situation in a FEEL GOOD way FOR

YOUR OWN SAKE, NOT THEIRS. Here is a formula for getting over anything that is hanging you up.

The Hang Up Exercise and the Understanding Game

I want to reiterate the power and importance of attending top class seminars and learning from great teachers and motivators. The weekend seminar I learned this at had about eighteen hours of training of which Kevin Trudeau did all eighteen hours of the training. The hang up exercise was less than 5 percent of the entire weekend, but it is the ONE sentence I got from that event that changed my life. Attending seminars live can be the most life changing experience ever even if you only get one good lesson from the seminar. First we need to define the hang up. Reframe the hang up. Find the good and then learn the lesson. This is a powerful exercise and an amazing way to live. The hang up is that I can't get my work done as these kids are driving me crazy. Let's reframe it. What if they just buried their mom and they simply are dealing with the worst tragedy a kid has ever had to deal with. The good is that the flight is only an hour. I can get done what I can get done and when I land I'll find a quiet place and in fifteen minutes can accomplish everything I can on this flight. I feel a bit sorry for these darn kids. The lesson is the next time I'm surrounded by screaming and yelling kids I should play the understanding game and allow them to be who they are, so I can be who I am.

1. Define the Hang Up
2. Reframe the Hang Up
3. Find the good
4. Learn the lesson

I remember an event in my life that I so wish I would have had this exercise for. It was almost twenty years ago and I simply laugh about it now. It was my daughter's first birthday and we decided to have friends over. My wife and I were new parents, working hard, entrepreneurs and financially not doing well at all. We had several businesses but the money was not flowing to us. With all of my best friends and my entire family over at my house, the police department showed up. The patrol car pulled in the driveway and my first thought was maybe my dog had got loose or something. We lived in a small town of about 2500 people. So everyone knew everyone. He walked over and said, "Dave, I hate to do this to you with all these people here, but there is a grocery store about two blocks from here. I said, "Yes." He said, "You wrote a check there for baby formula and some other things and it came back on an account with no money. I'm sorry, but I have to arrest you and take you to jail for writing that check." Imagine the feeling. My heart sank, I was embarrassed, I was scared, confused, mad, and every other negative emotion you can imagine. So I was arrested, went to the jail, got booked and then my wife came and bailed me out. I was so mad at that officer. I was mad at my wife. I was mad at everything.

The challenge with an event that hangs you up is that if you don't get un-hung up then it can follow and affect you a long time. Every time you think about it you start attracting like experiences. That is how it works! That is the law of attraction. That is why this exercise of getting over the hang ups is so important. Another way of thinking about it is to play the Understanding Game. Set yourself up to win and feel good in every situation.

Define the hang up. I was arrested at my house in front of my family and friends for writing a bad check for baby formula.

Reframe the hang up. The police officer was just doing his job, and he tried to be very nice about it. I bet everyone sitting at the party has been in embarrassing situations just like me. My family loves me regardless and I'm sure they will laugh about it. We needed the baby formula and groceries. This just shows me that I need to make more money. By knowing what I don't want, I now know what I do want. This was a good thing.

Find the good. At least it happened in my small home town so I didn't actually have to sit in jail. It also really just affirms that I need to make more money and I'm sure I'll come up with a really good idea to get me out of this place in my life. I've just become relatable with a lot more people. My daughter is only one…she will not remember her dad being arrested at her birthday party.

Learn the lesson. Things like this happen every day in life. Fortunately when hang ups happen in my life I get to learn something and grow from it. I know I need to get my finances up and I'll watch my checking account better. I know I don't want to experience this again so I'll do better.

Like I mentioned before, there is nothing wrong with hang ups or negative emotion. It's only bad when you stay there and think about them constantly. By playing the understanding game like the man on the airplane with the screaming kids, or using the exercise to dissolve any hang up at any time, you are not stuck. Negative emotions and hang ups make you feel bad, right? What is the true end goal? Feel good is the goal, everyday every hour and every minute. So hang ups and negative feelings are simply indicators to let you know that you are not on the path to what you want. They are an alarm to you internally that you are not attracting what you want. Have you ever been asleep and woke to the most annoying sounding alarm clock and you just lay there and don't turn it off? This is what negative feelings are, an alarm. Just don't lay there your entire life and listen to them. Once you are aware of that you don't have to spend years getting over a hang up like most people. You can get over it in a matter of minutes.

Some people sometimes say, "But Dave, you don't know how serious this situation is." I can assure you that you are making it much bigger than it is. Think back to a terrible situation that happened five or ten years ago…when you sit around and talk about it what do you do? You LAUGH about it! Why wait ten years to get over something…just laugh about it now. Remember, your mind doesn't know the difference between what is real or imagined. You have not even let any fat accumulate on your mind. You are feeling good which means you are attracting the things you want. How do you know the things you want? That is what Mindweaving does. It helps to clarify exactly the things that fire you up!

When my brother committed suicide it rocked my world. I had learned these things at that point in my life, I simply was not applying them. Fortunately I had a mentor that took me by the hand, and I had a wife who believed in me unconditionally. I can honestly sit here today and tell you that I have actually found the good in my brother's tragedy. I have learned the lesson and certainly have reframed it. I can talk about it to anyone. The event still happened, I'm not saying you ignore it, that won't work, that just makes you think about it more. I'm talking about strategically removing the negative aspects of the event from your mind. That is what the Hang Up exercise will do. My dad used to spank the heck out of me and I probably deserved it! But this made me bitter sometimes towards my dad. I have used this hang up exercise on so many things in my life. I know my dad whipped me with a belt on many occasions and this could make me distant from him. I know my dad grew up with the same kind of dad, whipping him with whatever was available at the time to try to teach a lesson. My dad didn't have this exercise or a mentor like me at that time, so it is exactly what he knew he was supposed to do to raise the best kid he could! He was doing it to make me a better person. The good is that it did make me a better person. I'm sure there are a dozen excellent attributes about me that I can attribute to how my dad raised me. It is why I still think of him of one of my heros still today. The lesson is to not judge someone's actions just based on your own feelings about it. My dad had reasons for doing what he did, and they were all based on making me a better person. This is one simple example of using the hang up formula to release some old mind fat you have lingering in that head of yours. That mind fat will hold you back. That mind fat, when you think about it over and over again, will simply attract more thoughts like it. We have all met someone that is full of hate. They simply are mean people and have nothing good to say to or about anyone. At some point in their life the fat deposit was made and they have never been able to get over it. They have never been taught how to. We simply never learn how to take five minutes and erase a lifetime of misery. It is that simple. Especially with a coach or friend that understands this. They hate, therefore they attract more hate. It is just how the law of attraction works.

    Let's use this on another real life scenario that happens to millions of people every day. How many people get mad at their boss? How many people talk behind their boss's back every night when they get home?

"You won't believe what happened today! He/she told me I wasn't working hard enough. Can you believe that gave Joe the promotion and not me?" Guess what? You are just going to keep attracting that same feeling every day no matter how nice your boss is to you because that is what you keep reliving and thinking about. How do we get over these daily things quickly so they don't affect us?

Define it. My boss is treating me unfairly, he gave away my promotion and it's making me mad.

Reframe it. I can't imagine the pressure that my boss is under. I'm sure he has a lot more responsibility than anyone can understand. Joe probably deserved the promotion. He has been working really hard. I really like my boss and Joe.

Find the good. This is going to make me really get better at my job. Joe needed the promotion and his family will be really happy. This is going to give me a drive like I have never had before. I also have a much better understanding, when I'm the boss, how not to act. There is a much better promotion around the corner.

Learn the lesson. Things in life sometimes happen that don't seem fair. It has nothing to do with me personally. It's just a situation that had to happen to make me a better person.

It doesn't matter if you believe yourself right when you say this stuff or not, your mind DOES NOT know what is imagined or real! It is going to treat it as truth! If the stove is red hot, do you have to touch it to make sure it's hot? Of course not. When you define the issue, reframe it, find the good and learn the lesson, you just saved yourself hours of distress and possibly years of heartache. FEEL GOOD NOW! That is the ultimate goal.

This is also a great way to get over fears you have. I used to have a terrible fear of the dentist. I hated going to the dentist. I hated everything about it. This was a hang up for me. Once I learned about Mindweaving and the hang up exercise I don't mind going at all now. I defined my hang up of the dentist which I associated with pain. I reframed it by knowing it makes me healthier, that they don't hurt people and have things so you feel no pain. I found the good by knowing I'd have healthy long lasting teeth and a great smile. The opposite of ugly gross broken bad teeth is not what I wanted. I also learned the lesson that so many fears I have are not fears at all. It's just that so many other people say they hate the dentist, I learned I did to. FEAR is False Expectations Appearing Real. There is no such thing as good or bad…it is our own thinking that makes it so. You need to start realizing that your life is a reflection of what you think about everything around you. The 21 Day Home Study Boot Camp will help you make getting over hang ups a habit!

Chapter 6

The Thinking Cure

Getting over hang ups is really a great exercise and way to live with the negative actions and events that happen in your life. There are things that are playing in your head over and over again that are just thoughts that are holding you back. We call these stop programs or hold patterns.

This subject could be a book all by itself it is so powerful. *The Thinking Cure* helps eliminate the negative programs that are running in your head. These are thoughts like: I'm afraid, I'm embarrassed, what will my friends say, you can't do it, what if you fail, don't you remember the last time, that will never work, who do you think you are…

There is a Mindweaving Re-programming flow chart available in the back of this book as well as free on the www.thethinkingcure.com website. This shows an example of how a thought gets achieved as reality or shut down by hang ups and bad programs. The picture of this chart may help you understand much better how you think.

Stop programs or holding patterns are programs that we created based on what an authority figure, an event, society or the media told us. We believed it and it is stopping us from moving on when we want to become more. I have heard so many professional speakers and teachers talk about these things in the past five years. I have read several books that talk about these negative programs, stop programs, bad programs or thoughts that are placed in your mind not by you. They are very real and they play over and over in your mind. They are like chatter going on and on and on. This will be the easiest exercise in the book. It is simple and profound, and the first time you do it you may actually feel things shift in your physiology. Don't let how simple this is define how powerful it is. I use this daily now that I learned a simple exercise. I remember right where I was sitting when it sank in of how important this process is in achieving the things you want. I had heard about it a dozen times, but not until, once again, Kevin Trudeau was teaching how to eliminate these programs did it really sink in. He was sharing how little things throughout your life can really hold you back. This exercise is one of the most important things as a student I ever learned.

I want to make a little side note here. I've used this information in this book and still am using it today, but I don't want you to get lost in an entire book. Mindweaving, as you will see in the last chapter takes fifteen minutes to do. *The Thinking Cure* takes literally a few minutes. I have done these things in my life and can quantify my successes. In other words, I'm not just telling you something to sound good. I'm telling you how a shy kid from western Kansas that quit college and went through some of the worst tragedies you can experience can build three different multi-million dollar businesses and counting. I'm telling you because I've overcome these things in my life. I'm tired of people falling out of relationships and struggling financially their entire lives because of some stupid program that some idiot put in their head. I've experienced these things first hand and certainly have walked the walk. I'm not some teacher that thinks he knows what is best for you, I was and still am a student that applied these things in my life and they worked so well I feel guilty if I don't share them.

These stop programs and holding patterns are real. You hear them throughout the day. You see a pretty girl or a cute guy and want to say hello. Immediately it plays. "Who do you think you are? You are not pretty or handsome, they will not talk to you. You're going to make a fool of yourself." You think of a great way to make some extra money and get yourself and your family out of a financial bind and the programs start playing, "Who do you think you are, you can't do that. That is a stupid idea, someone already tried that…"

There are two ways to eliminate and make these programs running in your head impotent.

Important point: These stop programs only affect the way you THINK not the way you FEEL. This is very important as there is no physiology behind these programs. They simply stop the way you think about something. They don't make you sad, mad, glad, jealous or anything else; they just STOP you from moving forward. They are very similar to hang ups, but where hang ups are real events that happened in your life, these are programs playing over and over in your head.

1. Eliminate them. That is very hard and takes a tremendous amount of focus and time. And while you are trying to eliminate them you are thinking about them so you in many cases just get more of them.

2. The best and most effective way to eliminate these stop programs in the fastest manner and make them impotent is to simply DISSOLVE THEM.

    You may say, "Dave, you just said these are programs running in my head and I'm not supposed to listen to them." You can't ignore them, because if you try to ignore them guess what, you are THINKING about them and will just attract more of them. Try this exercise. DON'T THINK OF AN ELEPHANT! What did you think of? I told you not to. That is how trying to ignore the things you don't want works. You just get more of it. There is a quick exercise that will dissolve these programs forever. I'm going to say it again. One day, maybe a hundred years from now people will look back and say, "I simply cannot believe they lived that way. If I had to mentally suffer like those people I would have killed myself." Think about that one.

    There is a simple, fun and extremely effective way to eliminate these stop programs that either you created or someone with authority, the media or society put in there. I have learned several different ways to eliminate these things in my life. The exercise explained in this book, in my opinion, is the easiest and most fun way to get rid of these bad programs.

>Acknowledge/Recognize
>Delete
>Replace

Here is how the exercise works. This is how you should do it. I want you to think of a little two inch troll man that is wearing a red hat. Yes, a tiny two inch troll, wearing a red hat. The next time you hear one of those thoughts playing in your head I want you to stop right where you are. I want you to imagine this troll talking to you about these things. (Dave in his very high pitched troll voice) "You can't do it, what if you fail, she will never talk to you, you are just going to embarrass yourself, don't you remember what happened last time, that will never work..."

Let the troll keep talking and then just simply say, "Are you done?" Then visually take your foot and squash the troll! It really is that easy! Look at the Mindweaving Reprogramming flow chart...this makes so much sense!

1. You are acknowledging and confronting the situation just like we do in the hang up exercise. We are defining the hang up or stop program. Up until now you have never had a way to dispose of these negative programs; they have controlled you and you may have even argued with them, which gave you MORE of them!

2. You are simply going to let the thought talk and talk, imagining it is a little troll with a red hat and then you are going to say out loud with a little force, CANCEL.

3. You are going to replace that program with a new decision and new program but with good feelings. This then tells your brain THIS is one of the thoughts to actually

manifest in the hundreds of thousands of meaningless ones buzzing around up there.

Let's look at a few examples. Once you get this you will not believe how easy it is. You will wonder why in the world people struggle so much and WHY NO ONE HAS EVER TAUGHT US THIS STUFF! This again is why the 21 Day Home Study Boot Camp is so powerful. It will help make squashing these bad programs a habit.

You are in high school and in speech class. You have to give a three minute speech in front of your peers. You are standing up front and you start, you forget some of the speech and some of them are laughing and snickering at you. Ten years later you are getting ready to speak in front of a few people in the front of the room on a stage or platform. You know what you are talking about as that is why they asked you to talk. All of a sudden the stop programs start. The troll says, "You are going to forget what you are going to say, they are going to laugh at you, why are you doing this…" What you need to do is simply stop, imagine the troll saying these things. Then ask the troll, "Is there anything else?" Then simply say, "Cancel and squash him." Now let's replace that old program with a new command. "You know, I do remember at one time in my life I was laughed at when speaking in front of a crowd. (we acknowledged it) It really made me embarrassed. But you know, I'm so excited to speak in front of these people. I have prepared my talk and I know how great this information is. Once they hear me they are going to be impacted. I know sometimes a person might get nervous before a speech, but what that really is, is just me wanting to give the best talk I can. I can see myself smiling and doing the best speech ever. I see the colors of the room I'm in and even can hear the people clapping."

You are riding your bike down the street and a small tiny dog comes barking like crazy at you and you crash your bike. You now hate tiny little loud barking dogs. You are actually terrified of them. Five years later you are riding your bike down the street and a little loud barking dog is running after your bike. The stop program starts to play. "Hey dummy, here comes that little dog that made you crash that one time. You're going to crash, he's going to bite you". Simply say to yourself as you are thinking that a little troll is telling you these things, "Okay, is there anything else?" Good, cancel. I know I don't hate little barking dogs. I just had one run out at me once and I crashed my bike. Actually little barking dogs are kind of cute. I may not like them enough to ever have one, but they are really okay. I actually have friends that have little dogs. I don't mind petting them and playing with them at all.

Acknowledge
Cancel
Replace

These are just a few examples but you will know when these programs start playing. This exercise is *The Thinking Cure*. You are eliminating all of the programs that are running in your head that keep you from achieving what you want. YOU ARE MAKING A DECISION to eliminate them by simply acknowledging them, cancelling them and then replacing that thought with a better command. "Oh my god I hate little barking dogs! I crashed my bike once because of one. Cancel. They are not that bad. That dog that day I crashed was a mean dog. Most little dogs are really okay. I don't mind them at all, I could see myself playing with a little dog."

When you make that decision you are basically playing the understanding game with the stop programs and hold patterns that are running your life. There may be hundreds of them too. Get in the habit of stopping when these thoughts come up and just taking two or three minutes and getting rid of them. Once you do they are gone. The negative energy is gone and eliminated. You just gave yourself a better command. You can do this with any thought during the day that puts you in a negative feeling. Have fun with this exercise and please share it with your kids if you have them. This is a great way to eliminate negative blocks in your life that maybe have been there for years.

There is a Mindweaving flowchart you can download at www.thethinkingcure.com that really shows this process of: Thinking a good thought and then a hang up stops you, fix it, think the good thought then a stop program stops you, fix it, then a good thought, then action, then a hang up, fix it, then a good thought, the action and the result. Most people never get past the first good thought unfortunately. This flowchart makes me understand so much more each time I look at it.

A Quick Recap

So what have we learned this far. First of all we have gone back in our minds and written down and thought about in detail great experiences that happened in our lives. At Mindweaving we call it G.E.T., Great Experience Thoughts. For some people this will take some time, but it is crucial to how fast your mind will grab onto the future things you want. Remember most of us are either afraid of the future or ashamed of the past, so just thinking about the things we want doesn't cut it. We need to remember what FEELING GOOD is all about! Some people have felt badly so long they forget how feeling good is. Remember when you watch someone talk about an old high school or childhood memory that they are proud of. Their face lights up, the physiology of their body changes and they feel good. Each time you G.E.T it…you get it! You are feeling good! That is the ultimate goal because that is when you create. Mindweaving simply makes sure you are creating what you want to be, do or have in your life.

Step one is to get those great past experiences going. The more in detail the better.

Step two is to go through the goal setting or dream building process. Where you actually write down and think about all of the things you would be, do or have if money and time did not matter. This process of dream building actually helps you define what you really want! Some people say, "Oh, I guess I want to go on a vacation." Do you really? Where? When? Who with? "I want to be a better person." What does that mean? How do you see yourself as a better person? When I sit and coach people and I start the dream building process, it is amazing how many people think they want something only to find out they really aren't that excited about it. Most of the time they are trying to live another person's dream and not their own. Mindweaving allows you to be selfish and be what you are supposed to be…a creator of good feelings.

Step three is to take the dreams and goals of what we want to be, do or have and actually attach good feelings to them. This is a form of pivoting. Another great way to help this is to get pictures of the things you want to be, do or have and put yourself in the picture! Taking any thought and attaching the good feelings to it. I'd love to go on a vacation.

Where? Oh I'd like to go on a Mexican cruise to Cozumel. I want to take my family. Why would this make you feel good? Can you imagine getting on the huge cruise ship with friends and family! Can you imagine what it will be like when the loud horn sounds on the ship and it starts to move! I've heard the food on the cruise ships is simply amazing and you can eat all you want and whenever you want. I've heard it's like a formal seven course meal every night with waiters and butlers and everything. I want to see the crystal clear water and the beach! This step has you attaching WHY you feel good when you think about this dream or goal. This step locks what you really want into your mind. It's no longer a wondering wish…you are now using the law of attraction to get what you want. You can use this on a personal level too. Say one of your goals is to be more of an outgoing person because you think you are shy. How would you feel if you were an outgoing person? Describe a few situations.

So we have thought of great experiences in the past, defined what we really would be, do or have and we have attached the good feelings to those things before we even physically have them. That is the order of Mindweaving. This is how we create and why we feel good all of the time. PAST SUCCESSES TIED TO FUTURE GOALS. This is a magic formula and it is so simple.

Also woven in Mindweaving is the hang up exercise and *The Thinking Cure*. If you are setting goals or thinking of something you really want to do like go on a nice vacation and you keep coming up with, "But I can't afford it, I can't get the time off." Then do *The Thinking Cure* real quick. "You know, I know in the past I have had times when I couldn't afford things. Cancel. Maybe I couldn't afford them back then, but now with everything I have going on affording a nice vacation will be a walk in the park. I can feel my feet in the hot sand right now." Plus, when you are Mindweaving and attaching feelings to what you want… many of those old programs are scared to show their face. Your mind doesn't know what is real or imagined, and if you have thought of what you want to be, do or have in complete detail, your mind thinks that is the norm and that is what you are supposed to have.

Chapter 7

Five Minutes to Learn and a Lifetime to Master

One of my mentors shared a statement with me some time ago. It is a ridiculously simply concept. All of the things in Mindweaving are easy to do. Everyone in the world can do Mindweaving. *The Thinking Cure* is the neatest exercise that anyone can do. You can learn it in five minutes, but it can take a lifetime to master. It is something you work on every day. It is someone you become. You are a Mindweaver…you feel good all of the time. You know if you aren't feeling good it's just your internal guided missile saying, "Hey! I'm not dialed in…get me dialed in. I don't just want to go with the flow of the world, that's not why I'm here. I'm here for you. So you can have, be or do anything and everything you want." You do not have to listen to the crap anymore. This is where the 21 Day Home Study Boot Camp can really help you make Mindweaving a daily habit!

I remember visiting with my mentor one day. I was frustrated in my business and I thought it should be going so much better. It was good, I was just stuck and it wasn't going up as fast as I thought. As we were visiting he simply asked me, "Dave, do you know what you want?" I was like, "Of course! I want this and this and this and this"…I just rambled. He said, "Do any of those things make you feel good?" We started going through the things I was hoping my business would do and only one of them really made me feel good. I was doing my business for the wrong reasons! How many of your have ever had an idea or something that "sounded" good and then nothing ever came of it? It is because we live by that sound in our head and not the FEELING inside. Once I got dialed in to why my business's success would make me feel amazing, my business took off. My wife and I actually were in a sales business together, and out of over 100,000 other sales people…we became the number one person in that company. I remember sitting at a huge convention in Chicago just eight months after my wife and I started our direct sales business together. We were having a very nice seven course meal as we had achieved a new level of success. Everyone at our table had been in the business for three years, five years, ten years and more. As we started to visit they had mentioned how young we were and how interesting it was that we were in the top ten percent of the company already. It was no surprise to Barb and I, we were surprised we were not in the top one percent yet! Even though they were top leaders all they did was sit at the dinner table that night and talk about what the company could have done differently, what was wrong with this and that and how things could just be so different to make it easier for them. I was amazed at their conversations! I NEVER thought any of those thoughts one single time in my eight months. Barb and I were dialed in. We had huge goals and pictures of the things we wanted to accomplish. We KNEW how those things would make us FEEL and there was no looking back. This simple attitude eventually not only took us to the top one percent but to the top money earners in that company. At the same time, those people at my dinner table stayed where they were and never grew or did anything else. We ALL had the same opportunity! Barb and I just thought about it differently. THAT IS THE ONLY DIFFERENCE! This was one of the first times in my life where I saw *The Thinking Cure* and Mindweaving work in a very big way. It made me financially free and I was certainly not used to that! Mindweaving works. Dialing into your guided missile works. Your internal system and mind is craving it. If you don't do this, then your mind will just accumulate the fat from the news, your friends, your parents, your spouse (which is why you and your spouse should do Mindweaving together), your school, your teachers, your church or any other person that is not you that you are hearing. Then think about it, what was the difference between Barb and myself, and all of the other leaders in that company? We had the same company, same products, same training, same everything except those leaders LISTENED TO EACH OTHER COMPLAIN AND STAYED STUCK THERE THE REST OF THEIR LIVES! That is a huge lesson I learned.

Practice does not make perfect…
Perfect practice makes perfect

What if I show you how to swing a baseball bat the wrong way? I put the wrong hand on top, I have you stand with your feet crossed and I have you swing straight down at the ball. Are you going to have any success? If you practice as hard as you can for the next three months, will you ever get better and hit the ball? No. Most of us have been "practicing" life and becoming everything we want to be, do or have the wrong way. We say all the time, "I just want or need more money dammit! I'm just so frustrated!" By the definition of the law of attraction, we just get more of those feelings and more of those experiences.

The phrase five minutes to learn and a lifetime to master fits here. That is so true in so many areas of our lives. Professional athletes that get paid millions of dollars do the exact same things that ten year old kids on the baseball field are doing. The professional athlete has it dialed in to his guided missile and has practiced over and over again the right way. It may only take five minutes to learn how to hold the baseball bat, but it takes a lifetime to master. He may have been holding it the wrong way, but a coach along the way corrected that and now he is practicing perfectly. Tiger Woods is dialed in to being a professional golfer. He does the same thing every other golfer in the world does, he swings at the ball and hits the ball. That is all golf is. He is taking a lifetime to master it as it is dialed into his guided missile. He doesn't care what anyone else thinks or what they are doing, he just plays golf and continues to master it. Every once in a while even Tiger Woods has a coach that is making sure he is swinging the club correctly. Once you start Mindweaving you will notice what others are saying and doing don't have anything to do with what you are doing. We will condense the Mindweaving process into a daily fifteen minute exercise at the end of this book.

Asking yourself important questions

First of all I want to be clear that as I share what other professionals, speakers and authors have done for me, I do so in a way that I hope you want to go and get their books and materials as I did and learn straight from them. I will add a list at the back of this book sharing some of my most favorite and most dynamic difference makers in my life. There is nothing like getting turned on to a new author or trainer, buying their book, and begging for it not to end. Mindweaving and *The Thinking Cure* are simply me being a student for twenty years in this classroom of life, learning how it works and most importantly applying it in my life. I am simply amazed at how few people know any of this amazing information and the ones that do know it…don't DO anything with it.

A good friend of mine came and spoke for me at one of my events. He actually owns a company called Freedom Personal Development. It is a company that helps empower people in truly leading edge ways. His name is Eric Platenberg. Eric is one of those friends that you may not visit with for a long time, but when you do the words are like gold. I remember him sitting in our suite after I had him come and speak at an event for us. He had just finished climbing Mount Everest and was just so in tune to everything around him. He spoke for us and did a tremendous job and then we just hung out. We had one of the best visits I have ever had. We sat up until 4 a.m. just chatting about life, success, the future and what our next steps were. I still value that conversation today as one of the best conversations I've ever had. He has the most unique way of asking powerful questions and then not saying a word, just listening. Eric was mentioning a few authors and recommending a few books to me as I had not heard of them. One of them was Dan Millman and *The Peaceful Warrior*. It was such a good book I bought three more, one for each of my kids. He also mentioned the book *Power vs. Force* by Dr. David Hawkins. I went immediately and purchased every book he mentioned that evening. Those hours visiting that night had a big impact on my making a decision to write this book.

Here is a big success principle. When highly successful people take the time to visit with you and talk about people and events that changed THEIR lives, you should be a sponge with a pen and paper and WRITE DOWN WHAT THEY SAY! Even though Eric is a friend, I still sat there taking notes. He mentioned a few authors to me that have made big impact on how I think today. One of the things I have consciously done in this book is to give you the best of the best in my mind. If you read a book and get one concept out of that book that you can readily apply in your life, then, grand slam home run! The people I mention in this book did exactly that to me. Thinking of Jim Rohn makes me think about the seasons of life and how there are always going to be different seasons in our life, but it is what we do and think about them that make the difference. When I think about Jerry and Esther Hicks and their visits with Abraham, I'm entrenched with the concept the law of attraction, pivoting, the art of allowing and getting in the vortex. When I think of Kevin Trudeau, one of my mentors and the best teacher I've ever listened to, I think of how to dream bigger than I ever have in my life and how ALL success principles only take five minutes to learn, but a lifetime to master. He taught me that everyone has OPINIONS but none of it is fact. Kevin taught me how to reframe things so that I always win. Once again, I'll give you my favorites list in the back of the book with the hope you find the same benefits I did from these amazing people. I have hundreds and hundreds of books between my office and home libraries. One of the reasons for writing *The Thinking Cure* and making it available to everyone is simply this…it is taking twenty years of personal development and giving you everything I've learned that has impacted me the most in the last twenty years. I literally have spent a small fortune in personal development, events, seminars, books, coaching and more. I became a very good student, then a sponge with a notebook and then applied them in my life. I want to give you the goods that have impacted me and share these people with you. More than that, I want to give you THE SIMPLE SOLUTION TO HELP YOU GET EVERYTHING YOU WANT IN LIFE! Mindweaving is using past successes, defining your goals of what you want to be, do or have and then focusing the good feelings on your future endeavors. Basically making you a magnet for the things you want.

Successful People DO What Others Won't

I remember the first time I was ever asked to speak. And I don't mean just some simple sales presentation that I had done hundreds of times already. I mean an actual keynote talk with a specific purpose and training in mind. My wife and I were cranking in our business and my mentor asked ME to go and speak to a group of HIS leaders. I was like, "Okay, why?" He said he wanted me to go and just share what I have been doing and in my mind why my wife and I had been so successful. Easy! I got on a plane, flew to South Dakota, got to my hotel room and started to think about the speech that was scheduled for the next morning. It was all pretty good until the next morning. I woke up early, walked around the hotel and went to the meeting room. I had been to a hundred hotel meeting rooms before, but not as the speaker! I was in the audience and a student. There were over one hundred chairs set up. I went back to my room and began to freak out! What was I doing there? Why would he ask me to do this? Doesn't he know I'm just some kid from western Kansas and I'm not a speaker? He is going to be so sorry. These people are not just my peers, I look up to them! Some of them are my mentors. And I have to speak in about 45 minutes. I really just wanted to throw up and go home! I still remember the color of the carpet in the meeting room, the color of chairs, where specific people were sitting. This was an experience that stuck with me and maybe helped make me the person I am today. I called my wife, said I was nervous as ever and just wanted to basically pass out or die. She said something to me that I still think about today. She said, "Dave, think about what it will feel like when you are all done and everyone has given you a standing ovation and can't wait to visit after the talk." That was all it took. I simply pictured me finishing the talk, thanking them for coming and I'd love to stick around and visit if they had any questions. It was one of the best talks and meetings I have ever done. Everyone applauded, several ask me if they could buy me dinner and everyone stayed after to chat. My point to drive home is this. How many times in your life have you thought a thought that is what you want or what you want to do and that judge or victim says, "Who do you think you are." The Mindweaving exercise is so powerful when it comes to following through on your everyday tasks that are making you better.

By simply thinking of the good, by simply feeling good even when you are in a difficult situation, you not only feel better…YOU ACT BETTER AND GET THE JOB DONE! How many times do people want to lose weight? They look at their body and say okay, I'm done. I'm ready to get a body I like! They are motivated and ready to lose weight. After about the third day of doing what it takes they are looking at the scale, looking in the mirror, feeling how their clothes still fit tight and just want to give up. Most do. You just need to hold that end result picture in your mind. Most of us can't do that because of all of the crap and fat already on our mind! Or you tell a friend you are going to trim down and they say, "Yeah right! How many times have you tried that?" When you are Mindweaving, you won't even hear your friends negative remarks, you will just know how good it once felt, what goal you have and how great it is going to feel when you hit that goal. Achieving goals can be as simple as just following through on a thought that makes you feel good. Most people quit, give up or stop way too early on the good feelings they have. It is like a pendulum swinging back and forth. When it's bad you just seem to attract more bad…but when it's good, it just gets better and easier so fast.

Chapter 8

How Do I Practice Perfectly Every Day?

Do you read a page or two at least of a good book each day? Have you been to a seminar to better yourself in the last few months? Do you listen to the radio in your vehicle or do you have some good CDs or audios of great speakers, teachers or authors? These are things that successful people do as a part of their daily lives. These are the things that most people never do. They are too busy, or too tired, or it doesn't pertain to them or more sadly, they simply don't know information like this exists. That should be a little bit of all of our goals, to give back and make sure people know that you can get great information and life advice on about anything. Mindweaving is one of the simplest things you can do every day to make a dramatic impact on your life. You don't have to go through life eating table scraps. You can order your life to be whatever you want. At *The Thinking Cure* we have a 21 Day Mind Makeover Boot Camp home action course that may be a good fit or good start for you. In twenty-one days experts show you can create and write an entire new habit on your brain. The home boot camp is designed to learn the habits of Mindweaving in any situation in your life. Mindweaving and feeling good just become a lifestyle for you. You simply won't accept anything other than to feel good in every situation. This is how the law of attraction works!

This is something that has been studied by religions, scientists, philosophers and great teachers everywhere. What is that something special that separates the top three percent to everyone else? Here is one thing they all agree on, it is inside of us all. You have that something special. All you have to do is release this power and get your mind in the habit of being successful! Yes, it is that easy. We at Mindweaving and The Thinking Cure are constantly giving you leading edge information. We enjoy sharing what we are learning. I encourage you to go to www.mindweaving.com or www.thethinkingcure.com and get on our email list. We have some great videos and training that break down everything in this book. And it is all on the website for free.

Awareness

Some people take what others say way too seriously and way too personally. This is an important lesson I learned that helped me in my Mindweaving every day. I was one of those people. I can remember early in my businesses when people would say something about my business or about me, I would take it so personally and also think they were probably right! What a big mistake. What others say is nothing more than their own opinions. When you are taking what others say too seriously that should be a quick gut check that is telling you that YOU ARE NOT DIALED IN to what you really want. If you were, what others are saying would never affect you. These are some of the things we really dive into at the Mindweaving Acadamy and Coaching Seminars. Self awareness is something you should kick in anytime something doesn't feel right. Self awareness is what should trigger *The Thinking Cure* every time a stop program pops up. Remember, your goal is to feel good all the time! That is what your internal guided missile is designed to do. When you are not going towards the things you want to be, do or have then your internal guided missile system has a way to let you know you feel badly. It is possible to feel good all of the time, and when you are, you are creating at a massive level. You are achieving everything you want and accomplishing more with the least amount of effort.

When others say something you don't agree with, or you hear something that the media has said that you don't like, try the understanding game and hang up exercise. It is magic. Sometimes you just have to LET other people be who THEY are so you can be who YOU are. You just have to ALLOW them to be themselves, believe what they want and live how they want to. It does not mean they are right or wrong, it just means that you don't agree with them and it has nothing to do with what is on your agenda. Remember, feeling good all of the time is the real secret. When you are feeling good you are attracting what you want. If you are thinking you are applying the law of attraction by thinking you need more money but deep inside you are fearful of all of the bills you have, you are just going to attract more bills. Does that make sense? You genuinely have to feel good in order to attract what you want. Mindweaving gives your mind the opportunity to do this.

Pain of Discipline or the Pain of Regret

This is where some of you might want a coach. Some of you can easily make a decision and set a goal and get it done. If you are like me, I needed a little coaching to just get me over that edge. How many of you know that you should be doing something but you simply won't do it. That is where a coach could help you. Even if it is ten to fifteen minutes a day to get you on track and to make you accountable, it keeps your guided missile moving. I had a few people that I considered my coaches. They were people who would keep me accountable and help me with any negative situations if they came up. They helped me with the hang up exercise anytime I had an issue, and within five minutes I eliminated things that could have hung me up for months. They helped me feel good all of the time! You are either going to suffer from the pain of discipline or the pain of regret. And the pain of discipline is really not pain at all, it is growth. Mental growth that removes the fatty negative junk from your mind just as running removes the fat from your body. Once you get in the habit of reading good books, listening to great teachers and speakers you won't want to stop! You just need to get in that habit. Once you start the Mindweaving process you will see how easy and fun it is. You will maybe for the first time in your life feel like you are in total control of your life. You will either go through life with unhappy and negative feelings that control your life, or you will discipline yourself to do the right things and experience the most fulfilling life ever. You do get to choose. Remember, success is a decision away!

The Disease of Mediocrity

This piece of history is worth doing your own due diligence and research. In the late 1920s and 1930s there was a man named Royal Raymond Rife. He had studied micro-organisms before anyone had ever heard of them. He developed his own microscope and could study the secret world of micro-organisms. With further research he was able to create and destroy disease causing organisms at will with electronically inducing the diseased organism with different frequencies. He was able to restore health to sixteen out of sixteen terminally ill patients…a 100 percent rate. All this was done without harming the person or the skin around the diseased area. He had discovered the ultimate weapon to control disease for all mankind. He was persecuted and betrayed to keep his discovery a secret. In the 1950s John Crane attempted to continue Rife's discovery and he was imprisoned. After reading books on Royal Raymond Rife one truly believes that there is a cure for things such as cancer and other diseases can easily be eliminated. This type of thinking has kept the human race in a state of mediocrity when it comes to understanding and maintaining good physical health. It seems there is a higher authority among people to keep the main population struggling. That has been true for all times. Kings, queens and royalty always had the best of everything while the rest of people did not. They had the best food, the best medicine and the best knowledge.

Around 400 B.C. there was a man named Socrates who was a great teacher. Still today there are books written about the thought processes and questions that Socrates posed to his students. He was known for simply asking questions until the answers came to be. He was put to death for this. He started asking questions and probing into why people are the way they are.

There are countless stories of how people have tried to make a quantum leap in human discoveries only to be put in prison or put to death for their work. It seems there is a disease of mediocrity that surrounds human beings. After hundreds and thousands of years of this type of thought and action, is it any wonder that we question ourselves when we have an idea. Is it any wonder that we question the mere thought that we COULD feel good all of the time! There have been studies after studies in quantum physics that attempt to find out why we are here? What are we supposed to do? How are we supposed to act? There is a great movie that all students should have to watch before leaving school. It is called What the Bleep Do We Know? It is a provocative movie giving insight on how we think. It shares on a quantum level what happens when we have a thought. It really allows you to understand that you simply can become what you think about.

We have stated before that the information in Mindweaving and *The Thinking Cure* are on the leading edge of thought. It is not that these things have not been thought of, it is that no one knows about them! Our mission and goal at our company is to share with people that they can have, be or do anything they wish in life. It starts internally, not externally.

Our mission at Mindweaving and *The Thinking Cure* is to show people that you can believe in your internal thoughts and wishes just as much as if not more than the external things you see with your eyes. Have you ever wondered why you believe in the building across the street but you don't believe you can be successful in a certain endeavor? You believe in what the weatherman's forecast but you don't believe you can find a fun spouse or partner? We believe in external things more than we believe in our own internal thoughts…AND THEY ARE REAL AND OURS! You do not have to live in so called mediocrity. Just as Napolean Hill said in his *Laws of Success* and later in *Think and Grow Rich*, "Whatever the mind of man can conceive and believe… it can achieve." It's just that simple.

Getting Rid of the Chatter

I can remember times in my life when I did ask important questions that were shrouded in either "I don't know" or "Why would you even ask that?" I can remember growing up in a church where there was one way to do everything. As I grew up I started to ask and think about why we are here? What are we supposed to do? Where do we go when we are gone? And no one could seem to even come close to answering any of these questions. I came to the realization after twenty years of personal development that FEELING GOOD is really our chief aim. When you feel good your body creates proteins that make you feel better. They create a chain reaction physically and actually start to give you more of what is making you feel good.

Think about a child that is five years old and knows he or she wants to be a doctor or a fire fighter. They know what they want! It makes them feel good. They actually PLAY out the things that make them feel good and we adults simply watch in awe. We certainly at times have said, "I wish I could be like that child. They know exactly what they want, they are so happy, they are so full of life." THEY ARE ACTING OUT WHAT MAKES THEM FEEL GOOD! If we adults sat around and did that publically they would lock us up. Think about it. Why does a drug addict become addicted? They are addicted to a FEELING, not the drug.

Fortunately as human beings quantum physics has determined that reality is what we see with our brains. Luckily, our brains do not know what is REAL or what is IMAGINED. Unfortunately most adults never imagine anything, they only live in the REAL world…the outside world that they can see and believe. Remember what Earl Nightingale said, "You become what you think about most of the time." The books *Think and Grow Rich* by Napolean Hill and *Psycho Cybernetics* by Dr. Maxwell Maltz both have entire chapters on how powerful and important a good imagination is.

In the movie What the Bleep Do We Know, they said our brains process over 400 billion bits of information every second. We are only aware of 2000 bits of information. Our brains, they stated, only lets us SEE what we believe to be possible! We create our own reality. We remember past experiences which lets us create and design our future that same way. How many times have you heard that we are just creatures of habit!

With that said: think of the following statements.

You become what you think about
The goal is to feel good all of the time so you can create good
Whatever the mind of man can conceive and believe it can achieve
Our thoughts create our reality

How Do I Practice Perfectly Every Day?

Pretty simple then! Just think of the good things I want to be, do or have and waaa laaa! I'm becoming what I think about and feeling good! That is in essence what *The Secret* and the law of attraction state. Simply think about what you want and you attract more of that in your life. So where is the hang up?

Our mind does not distinguish between good and bad. It allows about 2000 bits of information into our awareness THAT WE HAVE KNOWN TO BE TRUE IN THE PAST. We believe what we have seen or imagined. The media has basically destroyed the ability to hold on to a good thought. It is very difficult to see or listen to any form of media without hearing about gloom, doom and things that we relate to, not a good feeling. We have friends and family that make sure if we say anything good they are sure to have a negative comeback. We simply resort back to what our brain thinks is reality which is our past experiences… mostly negative.

Think about a magnet. If you put two opposite ends of a magnet together you get massive resistance. You simply cannot touch the two magnet ends together. It is good vs. bad, positive vs. negative, and they just don't mix. Scientists still have a hard time telling us why in the world two small magnets cannot be touched together on certain ends.

You have a great idea or have a goal that just makes you feel amazing. You then share it with someone that doesn't share your same feeling. It is like the magnet, the two ends are never going to see eye to eye. When you are a child it is usually your parent, teacher or family that will either laugh at you or think they are being honest with you about the goal you have.

Do you know how much work that would take?
Do you know how much money that would cost?
Do you know how much school and education you
 would have to have?
Don't you know there are not very many people that do that?
Why don't you get your head out of the clouds and
 get back to REALITY!!

Whose reality? Please ask yourself that then next time you have a negative feeling. Whose reality is creating this feeling? It's time for *The Thinking Cure*.

You need to have a filter to consciously get rid of the muck and junk that you run into everyday with the media, people around you, co-workers, parents, friends and just society as a whole. That filter is what mindweaving is all about. I share all of this quantum physics information just so you may ask yourself and search a bit yourself. Success is just a decision away, period. Once you make that decision you stick to it. That is where Mindweaving at *The Thinking Cure* will assist you in staying on track.

Remember, you become what you think about most of the time. If you hang around people that bitch, complain and always find the bad in things, you will too. That is what your mind sees as reality and the law of attraction will do exactly what it is supposed to do and give you more just like it!

I remember so many things as a child, teenager and then an adult that really made me feel good. Goals that made me so excited about life. And I can also remember the people that told me things like, "Why would you think you could do that," "Who do you think you are," "Don't you know what it takes to do that?" I have had a lot of dream and goal stealers in my life as I'm sure you have too. The exercises in Mindweaving and *The Thinking Cure* assist you greatly in allowing others to be who they are. They assist you in dialing in to exactly what makes you feel so good. And it assists you in attaching GOOD feelings to the things you really want which your brain in turn looks at now as REALITY. Your goals are now one of the 2000 bits of information that you are thinking about all of the time! The muck and negative are simply the billions of bits of information that roll of your mind like water off a ducks back. You are now creating what you want.

Let's recap:

Many of the books I have read talk about what it takes to make something a habit in ones' life. I'm not only taking what they say is true, but I've done this enough times in my life that I know this works. It

How Do I Practice Perfectly Every Day?

takes about twenty-one days to make the neurons in your brain fire and re-align with other neurons that eventually create a habit in your mind. All of us know how hard habits are to break. Well, they are, they are electric writings on your mind. What if we just develop good habits? That is a big part of Mindweaving and *The Thinking Cures* seminars, events, coaching and home study programs are about. Making you accountable until the things you really want to be, do or have become a habit in your life!

Now let's recap one more time the steps in Mindweaving so you can see how truly powerful they are. And more importantly than seeing, but believing that if you do them they will work.

1. Go back in your life experiences and start to pick out the good ones. We want to spend a little time writing down things that have happened to you in your life that just made you feel so good, so proud, so unstoppable…G.E.T (Great Experience Thoughts)

2. We now want to go through the dreambuilding process. We want to take some time and write down the things that we want to be, do or have in our life. What material things do I want? What person do I want to become? Are there characteristics that I have that I'd like to change (I'm shy and I want to be more outgoing)…

3. We now re-write these things but in much more detail.

4. We now write out these things, but this time attach the good feeling that we would have when this experience comes to be.

Of course woven in the Mindweaving exercises are the powerful pivoting exercise as well as the hang up and understanding game that help you understand what the negative things mean in your life and how to take advantage of them. Mindweaving and *The Thinking Cure* give you a simple way to use past good experiences to create a future life that you design. It is a mental workout to trim the fat from your mind.

Chapter 9

How to Mindweave and Put It All Together

When I am walking down the street or driving in traffic and someone cuts me off I have two choices. One, I can cuss the person out, scream at them from my car and really get mad. This will only make me not feel good and take me further from who I want to be and what I want. THAT IS THE LAW OF ATTRACTION. If you do this, don't wonder why you get in a fender bender in the next few days. Two, I can simply say, "Wow! That guy's wife must be having a baby! I better get out of the way so he can get there. I sure hope he makes it in time." Do you see the difference? It is a lifestyle, a way of life. To think good thoughts and feel good all of the time can be a way of life. It can be your lifestyle. The above example is a perfect example of getting over a hang up. There are people I know that if they would get cut off in traffic they would go crazy! I used to be that guy! They would come to work and talk about it all day. They would tell everyone in the office, then tell the mailman and then go home and tell their family. The problem with that is they are only going to attract more of that feeling and they will get more experiences just like it in their life. Tomorrow someone will cut in front of the line in front of them or take their parking spot! It is an endless cycle that can be fixed and erased in a matter of seconds. Getting over hang ups and playing the understanding game should become a way you think.

Using *The Thinking Cure* to acknowledge, replace and cancel past and current negative programs can save you years of negative miserable feelings. AND IT'S FUN WHEN YOU START DOING IT!

The ultimate goal is that you read the book, maybe watch the videos online, attend a few seminars and listen to the audios as much as you can the first twenty-one days. Maybe you are pretty goal oriented and the 21 Day Home Study Boot Camp would get you on track. Taking some time to do the exercises in this book or online can get you feeling good. This book is designed to take how we think as a human being, how we accomplish things that are real that we see and believe in our everyday lives and then attach that same power and thinking to future goals so our minds don't know the difference between the good things we have done and the good things to come.

Fifteen Minutes a day

Once you understand how this works and you are dialed in to your guided missile it is just a matter of feeling good all of the time! Mindweaving for five or six minutes twice a day will do wonders in your life. Following is a typical six minute session. You can do it silently or you can certainly do it out loud. I encourage you to do this right at bedtime and again right when you wake up. If you want to take an afternoon break great, but once you have gone to bed and woke up doing this you are good. You also should use the exercises that you have written down and read them the first few times or every time for all that matters. After you start to do this you will know exactly what you want and how this works. I hope you are like me and become addicted to Mindweaving.

First two minutes: During the first two minutes of your Mindweaving you are simply going to do nothing but think of the greatest past accomplishments in your life. If you need to read them the first few times that is fine. You want to get to the point that these are so vivid in your mind that you can feel yourself experiencing these things all over again. We have stated in the book to get very detailed. The more detailed you are in Mindweaving then better it will work. For two minutes you are going to just think of how good you are, the things in your life that have made you feel the most amazing and the experiences that made you feel like a king or queen. Maybe your wedding, the day you first learned to drive, a special day with a parent, the day a child was born, a time in business when you were recognized for your achievements, someone you look up to who said something nice to you, the play that won the game, the first time you kissed your girl or boyfriend…

Next two minutes: During these next two minutes you are just going to think about the things you want. If it is a new house then think of the new house. This is why getting pictures of the things you want can be so powerful. I've coached people and have asked hundreds of times, "Where are your pictures?" They didn't think that step was important. It is. These two minutes you just think of the top one to three goals on your list. If you just focus on one in the morning and one at night that is best, but you can certainly think of more than one during these sessions. Just go down your list of goals during these two minutes and think about them. If it is new car then what color, what brand, get detailed. If you are shy and you want to be more outgoing then think about what your face would look like, what your attitude would be, what would you be wearing? Are you single and want that perfect mate? What are they like? Get detailed about the things you want to be, do or have the most.

The final two minutes: During these two minutes, you are going to take each one of the goals you just thought about and attach a feeling to it. How does it feel when you walk in your new home? How does it feel when you drive away in your new car? When you find that perfect mate how do you feel? Again, the more detailed the better.

Then for eight or nine minutes just sit or lay in complete silence. So many teachers and leaders talk of the power of going into the silence. Many religious leaders including Jesus mention many times to go into the silence and dark when you are asking for guidance and the things you want. Some people call this meditation. I like the phrase going into the silence as it reminds me to be quiet, to let everything go that I have been thinking about and just let my guided missile do the work it was designed to do. Let those programs re-write themselves.

Throughout the day make sure and smile and acknowledge when things happen in your life that are in direct relation to your Mindweaving sessions! Appreciate the fact that you know you are creating the things you want to be, do or have.

Mindweaving and *The Thinking Cure* have many different delivery methods to assist you in making this a habit so you can truly feel good all of the time. During the day negative things may cross your path and the quicker you learn to eliminate their energy the better. It is not just ignoring them, most negative things that happen are very real, but you can certainly change the way you FEEL about them. These exercises keep you on the path for twenty-one days to change those neurons' paths in your mind to attach the things you want to good feelings. That is the magic.

Nutrition and Physiology

I remember a talk that Jim Rohn was giving one time. He said, "Sometimes people don't do well because they don't feel well." It's not very often that we attach our mental states and the success we have in our lives and how we feel every day to our nutrition. I encourage you to start to do the right things if you already don't. Getting the right amount of sleep, drinking plenty of good water and putting the right foods in your body can make a tremendous impact on your life. There are so many great programs out there that focus on doing the right things to your body. Exercise a few times a week and you will start to have more energy than ever before. Pay attention to what you put in your body and take a little time to learn a little bit about nutrition. Hit the library or internet and see how important water is to your body. There are some great things you can do physically that will make a difference mentally. We talked a lot about food for your mind in Mindweaving, but taking care of your body is just as important. In quantum physics, though, many scientists believe you have actual power and energy in your mind to affect the physiology of your entire body by simply having the right thoughts. I'll let you think about that one.

My Wish for You

I was sitting in Kansas City, Kansas at the Marriott Hotel on Metcalf Avenue in 1996. That was the first time I attended a seminar of any kind.

How to Mindweave and Put it All Together

I sat in the crowd with a baby carrier on my right and my wife holding our other child on my left. When the speaker came out and started to talk about dreams and goals and how anyone can achieve whatever they want in life, I was hooked. I had never heard anything like it. I've been hooked for over twenty years. It still amazes me today of how few people work on their mind at all. We pay five bucks for a cup of coffee but won't get on a great monthly program for two dollars a day that can change your life. I'm so grateful my mentors drove this point so deeply into my mind. As Jim Rohn says, "You need to work harder on yourself than you do on your job." That is magical. Or how my friend Charlie "Tremendous" Jones said to me many times, "You will become like the people you meet and the books you read."

My wish is that you get on a great monthly training program. We offer a fantastic one at *The Thinking Cure*, one is free and one costs, just find one you like and get on it. We at some point as a human species have to start to truly look out for one another. We have to start to share the great discoveries like Royal Raymond Rife has discovered. We need to learn to be 100 percent unselfish and cheer our fellow man on and honestly wish him or her the greatest success ever. At some point, politics, religion, bickering and fighting for who's right must stop. We are human beings. We are better than that. We are champions inside. That is our birthright and it is time to claim it.

Mindweaving and *The Thinking Cure* were started so you don't have to wait twenty years to experience some of the amazing revelations I have. I encourage you to get on that journey of personal development and become as addicted as I. I hope you reach so many goals, become the person you want to be, see the world for what it is instead of a pool of murder, rape and crime as the media portrays and share the great feelings you have with the ones you love. We all have a choice every waking moment to be happy, glad and feeling good or angry, sad and miserable. *The Thinking Cure* makes feeling good a lifestyle, a way to live.

I hope you find the answers to these questions when you look up in the amazing sky at night…

Why are we here?
What am I supposed to do?

Where am I going next?

And when you find them…please share them. There are millions of people lying awake tonight struggling with things in their head…let's help them. Let's spread the word of *The Thinking Cure* and let's LEAD BY EXAMPLE! Start to apply this in your everyday life and you will be a living example for people to see that they too can achieve all they want to in their life. People will see you as the person that everything you touch just turns to gold. How you act, speak and live will speak louder than anything else you could do.

FROM THE AUTHOR

The day that anchored my mission happened as I was speaking at a weekend event and I had about an hour to share. I talked about dreams and goals and why most people don't achieve them, in my opinion, and I also shared briefly the exercises with *The Thinking Cure*. A few hours later the event was over and I was meandering around with everyone that attended the event. People were coming up and saying how much they appreciated the insight. Each time someone would come up and introduce themselves to me I kept seeing a guy about my age keep looking at me from about twenty feet away. When our eyes would meet he would look away really fast. This went on for about 45 minutes. I would meet a few people and he would just be standing there. When the crowd had thinned out he eventually made his way over to me. I didn't recognize him at first but we had actually gone to school together. He asked if I remembered him and I said of course. He then went on to share a little of his life with me. He said, "Do you remember all of the fights I got into in school?" I really didn't know what to say. He told me that he was the kid that always got teased. He was the kid that always was made fun of. He asked if I remembered that one fight that he had got in right in front of the school. He relived it like it had just happened and it was over 25 years ago. He went on to share that he remembered that I was always really nice to him and that is why he actually came to the seminar. His eyes started to tear up and he said to me, "I have a lot of challenges and issues in my life and I still think of those horrible days in school." He went on to share that this was the first time anyone had ever shared with him that all of those negative things that happened could be dealt with and eliminated. With tears in his eyes he said he could actually see himself setting goals and getting out of the negative situations he was in. He had hope. I didn't notice, but when he walked away my wife walked up to me and asked if I was okay. I told her sure, why do you ask? She said, because you have tears running down your cheek. I was crying and didn't even know it. I have those same tears in my eyes right now as I write this. He had been reliving terrible things that happened over 25 years ago every day of his life.

People out here in the real world have struggles. Struggles that just some positive mantra is not going to do anything for. I had struggles and fortunately had a teacher and mentor THAT TAUGHT ME TO DREAM! I was not only taught to dream, but how to handle the real issues in life in a way that still kept me on course to achieve what I wanted. Too many people are just wandering around in a coma with no hope and have been reliving things that happened 25 years ago. You are not going to attract or accomplish many of the things you want with that type of thinking. You are not helping anyone either by staying in those same old negative thought programs. You are better to everyone around you when you are happy and feeling good. My old classmate that day showed me how much of a passion this stuff is to me. I was a student for twenty years and applied these things in my life. I still do apply them everyday. I still have struggles like everyone. I just don't let them last but more than a few seconds though, not 25 years. *The Thinking Cure* and Mindweaving is my lifestyle. I live it. I want to invite you to do the same.

I truly hope you are inspired and follow through on the exercises and make Mindweaving a lifestyle choice. I encourage you to visit www.thethinkingcure.com and download the free videos, audios and the free coaching. We give away some terrific insight and really want to be a beacon to help people stay at the right depth so they can achieve and become all they can be. It is so often that someone sets a goal that very quickly just becomes a wondering thought. Tune into the videos on the website, share them with anyone you feel could benefit.

We also love the energy of live seminars and events. If you have a group or company that you feel could benefit by learning the art of Mindweaving in a live setting contact us. Live seminars are so much fun! You can watch someone on a cruise ship on TV, or you can be on the cruise ship in person…there is a difference. If you can get to one of the Mindweaving Academy seminars it will be well worth the effort, time and money invested.

There is also a fantastic home Mindweaving Boot Camp. This is a twenty-one day program to get you to simply make Mindweaving a part of your everyday life by habit. Check out the website and see what fits best for you…but most importantly, DO SOMETHING! Make feeling good, achieving everything you want and becoming the person you want to be a lifestyle that you subscribe to.

Until we meet…
Keep your DREAMS Alive!!!
David Pitcock

To contact David or inquire about David speaking for your organization or company and help them with Mindweaving go to www.thethinkingcure.com

Visit www.thethinkingcure.com or email David directly at david@thethinkingcure.com to see what seminars, workshops and retreats are available to attend.

The Thinking Cure has recently released a 21 Day Home Study Boot Camp course that takes you through the entire Mindweaving experience from home. There are also personal coaching opportunities with David on the 21 Day Home Study Boot Camp.

You can also mail to:

The Thinking Cure
125 East 7th Russell, KS 67665

The Thinking Cure

Below is a representation of an example of why so many thoughts that you think are great ideas, or truly things that you really want to be, or have never happen. Mindweaving helps reprogram these hang ups and stop programs.

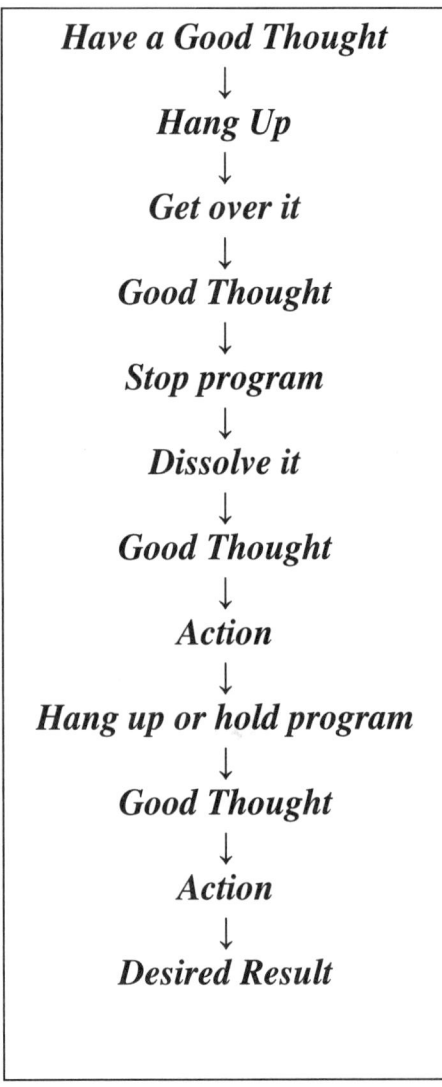

Have a Good Thought
↓
Hang Up
↓
Get over it
↓
Good Thought
↓
Stop program
↓
Dissolve it
↓
Good Thought
↓
Action
↓
Hang up or hold program
↓
Good Thought
↓
Action
↓
Desired Result